SUNRISE BRANCH

Regina Public Library

Library materials are loaned for the period marked and only on presentation of a library card.

Please report change of residence promptly.

Card holders are responsible for loss, damages and the prompt return of all books, records, films, pictures or other library materials marked out on their cards.

HOLIDAY BOOKS

CANADIAN CHRISTMAS STORIES

Acknowledgements

"The Christmas Cactus" by Don Bailey is reprinted from *How Will We Know When We Get There?* (Mosaic Press) by permission of the author. "The Santa Claus Trap" by Margaret Atwood is reprinted from *The Weekend Magazine* by permission of the author. "The Three Christmases" by Marian Engel is reprinted from *The Weekend Magazine* by permission of the estate of Marian Engel. "Christmas Under a Pale Green Sky" by Barbara Novak is reprinted from *Who and Why* by permission of the author. "The Wounded Christmas Choirboy" is reprinted from *Vibrations in Time* (Mosaic Press) by permission of the author and the Robert Drake Agency. "A Migrant Christmas" is reprinted from *Chatelaine* and *Inland Passage* (Lester & Orpen Dennys Limited) by permission of the author and Georges Borchardt Inc. "One More Wiseman" by David Helwig is reprinted from *The Toronto Star* by permission of the author. "Christmas at the Crompton" by David Cavanagh is reprinted from *The Whig-Standard Magazine* by permission of the author. "The Bird Feeder" by Donna Gamache is reprinted from *Our Family* by permission of the author. "On Christmas Eve: 1963" by Joan Finnigan is reprinted from *I Come from the Valley* (NC Press) by permission of the author. "A Christmas Story" by Roy Bonisteel is reprinted from *The Whig-Standard Magazine* by permission of the author. "Upon a Midnight Clear" by Margaret Laurence is reprinted from *The Weekend Magazine* and from *Heart of a Stranger* (McClelland & Stewart) by permission of McClelland & Stewart, The Canadian Publisher. "Boxing Day" by Linda Svendsen is reprinted from *Northwest Review* by permission of the author and the Robin Straus Agency.

CANADIAN CHRISTMAS STORIES
in Prose & Verse

EDITED BY DON BAILEY
AND DAILE UNRUH

QUARRY PRESS

The publisher thanks The Canada Council and the Ontario Arts Council for assistance in publishing this book.

CANADIAN CATALOGUING IN PUBLICATION DATA

Main entry under title:

Canadian Christmas stories in prose & verse

ISBN I-55082-001-X

1. Christmas — Poetry. 2. Christmas — Fiction.
3. Canadian Poetry (English) — 20th century.
4. Canadian fiction (English) — 20th century.
I. Bailey, Don. II. Unruh, Daile.

PS8237.C57C361990C811´.5408´033C90-090423-2
PR9194.5.C53C36 1990

Cover art entitled "Christmas Trees" by Hazel Bosley from *French Canada: Pictures and Stories of Old Quebec.*

Imaging by ECW Type & Art, Oakville, Ontario. Printed by Hignell Printing Limited, Winnipeg, Manitoba.

Distributed in Canada by University of Toronto Press, 5201 Dufferin Street, Downsview, Ontario M3H 5T8, and in the United States of America by Bookslinger, 504 North Prior Avenue, St. Paul, Minnesota 55104.

Published by Quarry Press, Inc., P.O. Box 1061, Kingston, Ontario K7L 4Y5 and P.O. Box 348, Clayton, New York 13624.

Contents

Preface

Christmas is celebrated by most of us in North America four days after the winter solstice. We are evolving from the darkest time of year towards the light. We celebrate the lengthening days and many of us reflect on how we have filled our time over the year that is nearly finished. Regrets are acknowledged and new dreams are born in an atmosphere of hope.

Christmas is a time to exchange gifts with those we care for, to reach out to those we have overlooked. It is a season to renew passions that have become buried and forgotten under the everyday grind of surviving.

During the Christmas season most of us strive to be better human beings. We tolerate relatives that we abhor around our feast tables. We sprawl on the living room floors with our children and allow them to show us how their new toys operate. Some of us become more physically demonstrative, hugging ancient aunts that have halitosis capable of melting plastic.

Christmas is an emotional territory, a kind of promised land where expectations are sometimes raised to unrealistic heights. So while for some it is a time of great joy and delight, for others it is a period in which they experience disappointment and sorrow.

In this collection of prose and verse we have tried to select writing that represents the many moods triggered by the Christmas season. We were surprised and pleased to find that even in the darkest tales, a glimmer of light shone through. That and laughter. And it is our hope that readers of this book will find something to nurture their hearts and souls.

Daile J. Unruh and Don Bailey

Christmas Cactus

DON BAILEY

These are not plants
I admire
for the feel of their
shape in my hands

these plants
are not meant
for touching,

but rather
they exist
as patterns,

like the marks
in your mind,

the culverts
carved by tears,

the fading foot-prints
of those who are always leaving,

and the finger-smudged pictures
of those you have loved.

these plants have a sameness
that is like the hurts
you have felt
and the wishes you have made.

and yet
this is the plant
I would give you before
all the others,
because like love
it bursts into bloom
at the oddest times
and produces
the most delicate
and beautiful of flowers.

The Santa Claus Trap

MARGARET ATWOOD

Once upon a time there was a man named Mr. Grate,
Whom the thought of Christmas filled
With an indescribable and fungoid hate.

He hated Christmas trees and presents
And carols and turkeys and plum
Puddings, and he thought Santa Claus and his reindeer
Were not only dumb

But ought to be banned and not allowed
Into the country, and dogs
That barked and children who laughed
Too much made him furious,
And he wished they would all fall down
Holes or drown in bogs.

Mr. Grate, although he was quite rich,
Lived in one miserable little room

Which he never cleaned with a vacuum cleaner
Or swept with a broom

So that it was all covered with dust and dirt
And spiderwebs and old pieces of cheese
And so was Mr. Grate,
And if you ever came near him
You would begin to cough and sneeze,

But nobody ever did, because he never went outside,
But stayed in,
And counted his money, and wrote nasty letters to the editor,
And sometimes drank a bottle of gin

All by himself, or a glass of lemonade without any sugar,
Because he liked it sour,
And he peered out the window and hated everybody,
By the hour.

He had round eyes like an owl's
And his face was all squizzled up
And covered with frowns and scowls.

One day in December, Mr. Grate thought up a horrible plot.
"Everyone," he said to himself — he talked out loud a lot —
"Has a lot of nice things, much nicer than anything *I've* got,

And every Christmas they give each other presents,
And nobody ever gives *me* none,
And not only that, but I never have any fun,

And Santa Claus comes and fills their stockings
And panti-hose and socklets

With oranges and licorice sticks and bubble gum
And chocolates.

But what if Santa Claus were to suddenly disappear,
And all that ever gets found is his empty sled and reindeer?
What if I could kidnap Santa Claus and keep him in a sack
And say I would never give him back

Unless the children sent ME all their candy
And jellybeans and maybe a teddy bear?
Not only would I get even with them and give them a scare,
But I'd have all the stuff, and maybe I'd even be a millionaire.

I'll keep Santa Claus in a cupboard
And feed him on water and crumbs,
While I sit outside and laugh myself silly
And stuff myself with candy apples and bubble gums!"

And for the first time in a long long while,
Mr. Grate began to laugh and chuckle,
But it wasn't a nice laugh, and he turned all red and purple
And rolled around on the floor
And had to loosen his belt buckle.

After that he got up again and set to work.
"The thing is," he said to himself,
"Santa Claus is obviously a jerk

All he ever does is give things to people —
It's really shocking —
And he can't seem to resist an unfilled stocking.

Therefore, all I have to do is get a lot of stockings,
And hang them all over the room as a kind of bait,

And build a trap in the fireplace which will catch him
When he comes down the chimney,
And then I'll just sit and wait."

So first Mr. Grate went to a Sale,
And bought a whole armful of stockings
And socks and mukluks and several rubber boots,
Pushing old ladies out of his way
And scowling and frowning at the men
Who were ringing bells, dressed up in Santa Claus suits,

And then he went to a junk yard and bought all kinds of junk:
Some pieces of old cars, a wringer washing machine,
Several rolls of barbed wire,
Some string and rubber bands, a wrench, a lever, a gear,
And a box full of old tin cans
Which unfortunately also contained a dead skunk,

But that's life, said Mr. Grate to himself
As he carted all these things home
In a U-Haul he'd rented.
And when he got them back to his room, he started to build
The most complicated trap that has ever been invented.

The trap was foolproof and full of pulleys and levers,
And anyone who came down the chimney and stepped into it
Would be grabbed by mechanical hands
And rollered on rollers and tangled in wires and zoomed
Right into a sack in Mr. Grate's closet,
And it looked as if Santa Claus was doomed,

EXCEPT

Next door to Mr. Grate lived some twins,

14

A girl named Charlotte and a boy named William.
Charlotte's favorite flower was the Rose,
And William's was the Trillium.

They were both very curious
And they were always looking in people's windows
And back yards and bureau drawers or over their shoulders.
Charlotte was somewhat self-contained,
But William was bolder.

And one day, when Mr. Grate was building his trap and
Talking out loud to himself
About his plan to hold Santa Claus to ransom,
Charlotte just happened to be standing on William's shoulders
And looking through his transom.

She overheard the whole plan, and she was so dismayed
She almost fell off,
And then she almost gave them away,
Because even Mr. Grate's transom was so dusty
It made her cough,

But luckily Mr. Grate was hammering something
At the time, and didn't hear.
Charlotte climbed down and whispered in William's ear,
"William, I have just heard the most terrible thing,
And Christmas is going to be ruined this year!"
These words of Charlotte's filled William's heart with fear.

The twins hurried back to their own house,
And sat down at the kitchen table,
And while they were eating some peanut butter sandwiches
To keep up their strength,
Charlotte repeated what she had heard, as well as she was able.

"But that's terrible!" said William. "If Santa Claus is caught
In the trap, and tied up with a large knot,

No children in the entire world
Will get anything in their stockings, you see!
And — I hardly need to point out —

That includes you and me.
I feel that this could turn into a major catastrophe."

"Don't be so obvious," Charlotte said.
"The main thing is, how can we stop him?"
"Well," said William,
"I could go over there with my baseball bat and bop him
On the head." "You aren't big enough,"
Charlotte said, she was practical.
"We have to think of a plan that is both feasible and tactical,

By which I mean something we can do ourselves
That will actually work."
But the possibility of no Santa Claus
Filled them with depression, gloom, and murk.

And they found it hard to even think about it,
It made them so sad.
"Some people are naughty," said Charlotte,
"but Mr. Grate is *bad*."

For days they did nothing but sigh and mutter
And eat sandwiches made of peanut butter.

Once they went to spy on Mr. Grate,
But the trap was even bigger,

And Mr. Grate was rubbing his hands
And looking at it, with a nasty snigger.

The sight of the enormous trap
Made Charlotte and William feel helpless and small,
And they seemed unable to think of anything to do at all.

They knew they couldn't tell the police or any grownups,
Because no one would believe them anyway,
And it was too late to write Santa Claus to warn him,
Because Christmas was due now any day.

"Is this the end?" said William, feeling doleful.
"Do not give up," said Charlotte, looking soulful.

AT LAST

They had a brilliant idea, and being twins
They had it both at once, because
Twins often do. "I know!" they cried together.
"We'll make a false Santa Claus!

We'll make it out of red potato sacks, and fill it full of rocks,
And let it down Mr. Grate's chimney on a rope,
And it will snarl up the trap and possibly break it, because
Of the rocks." This idea filled them with hope.

"Come on," said William, "let's get going,
We have no time to waste!"
So, pausing only to eat one more small sandwich each
And to put on their winter coats
And their mittens, boots and hats,
They rushed out the door in considerable haste.

"Where are they going?"
Their mother called after them as they ran down the street.
"We're going to save Santa Claus!" they called back, and
Not realizing the seriousness of the situation,
She said, "Isn't that sweet."

It was Christmas Eve, and Mr. Grate
Had hung up his stocking, or I should say
His stockings, because he had about a hundred of them
Dangling all over his room,
In every color you can think of,
Red, green, yellow, purple, blue, and gray,
And the total effect would have been rather joyous and gay

If it hadn't been for the sinster machine
Lurking near the fireplace in the corner.
"All right, Santa Claus," muttered Mr. Grate,
"Once down that chimney and you're a goner!"

He was sitting in his one dingy old chair,
Hugging himself and chortling,
When up on his roof he heard an odd sound,
Part scuffling and part snortling.

"It must be a reindeer!" cried Mr. Grate, and jumped up
To give the final touch to his arrangement of socks.
(It was actually Charlotte and William,
Having a little trouble with the rocks.)

"Now Santa will slide down the chimney
With a nice, round, fat kind of slither,
And I'll have him safe in my closet,
And all the children of the world will be thrown into a dither,

And serve them right," said Mr. Grate.
He could hardly wait.

But imagine his surprise
When instead of a round little man landing
With a comfortable plop in his trap, there was a loud crash!
Followed by a thud and a rattle and a smash!

Someone — or something — dressed in red
Had come down the chimney, though it wasn't light

Enough to see clearly, and Mr. Grate's trap had spun into action,
But it was throwing out sparks left and right!

Its mechanical arms were getting all snarled up
In the barbed wire,
And its washing machine wringer was out of control,
Spinning higher and higher,
And something seemed to be wrong
With the sack that Santa was supposed to fall into —
It had caught on fire!

Suddenly all the fuses blew,
And a thin, tiny, eerie voice came wafting
Down the chimney flue:

    "Mr. Grate! Mr. Grate!

    REPENT

    Before it is too late!"

This was actually Charlotte,
Which Mr. Grate had no way of knowing.

"It's ghosts!" he cried.
"I've got to get out of here, even though it's snowing!"

He ran towards the door, but because
There were now no lights in the entire place,
He tripped over something and fell flat on his face.

Then something else grabbed him from behind,
And one of the gears that wasn't broken began to grind,

And then there was an unpleasant ZAP
And Mr. Grate was caught in his own trap!
"Help, Help," he cried, and began to struggle,
Which only made the tangle worse,
"I'm perishing! I'm expiring!
I need a doctor and also a nurse! O curse

The day I decided to trap poor Santa Claus!
Please, someone, bring some wire clippers and tinsnips,
And wrenches, and saws
And get me out!"

Charlotte and William, on the roof, heard his feeble shout.
"I believe it's worked," Charlotte said. "He seems to be caught,
Which is more than we expected.
Should we let him out, or not?"

Mr. Grate was lying all covered with barbed wire
And bits of cheese from the floor,
And feeling decidedly sorry for himself,
And also rather battered and sore,
When Charlotte and William climbed
Through the transom over his door.

(They didn't have a key, and the door itself was locked.)
"Well," said Charlotte, looking down at Mr. Grate,
Where he lay clinking and clanking,
"In my opinion you deserve a good spanking."

"In *my* opinion," said William,
"You deserve a good kick in the behind."
"But," said Charlotte, intervening —
She felt one should be polite, if at all possible —
"This is Christmas and we are going to be kind.

We'll get you out of the trap *this* time,
If you promise not to do it again, and make amends."
"But why did you think of such an evil thing to do
In the first place?" said William.
"Boohoo," said Mr. Grate, "I don't have any friends,

Or a teddy bear, or *anything*,
And everyone else was having such a good time,
Especially at Christmas, and my room is all covered with grime,
And no one invites me to dinner,
And I never get anything in my stocking but pieces of coal,
Or sometimes a hole,
Or a rotten potato, and once, in a good year, a single Smartie,
And it's a long long time since I even went to a birthday party!"

"There, there," said Charlotte, wiping away his grubby tears,
While William was snipping him out of the trap
With a pair of shears,

"I understand perfectly. You just wanted some attention."
(Which had been said to her on several occasions
When she herself has been rather surly,
But these we won't mention.)

"You can come back to *our* house for Christmas.
I'm sure our Mum won't mind, if we ask,
And we'll even help you clean up your room."
Which they did, and it was an unpleasant task . . .

But in Mr. Grate's closet they found a couple of suits
That weren't too dirty,
And when they had washed his face and shined his boots

He looked quite presentable,
And was so pleased he actually smiled
And allowed his fingernails to be cut and his moustache filed,

And off they all went to Charlotte's and William's house,
And had a wonderful Christmas dinner
With lots of trimmings,
And when Mr. Grate got up from the table
He was certainly not thinner.

And after that day, though he was not
A completely different person, and still
Didn't like dogs much, and was known to spill

A few bits of cheese on the carpet now and then,
He was much nicer than before,
And played Monopoly with Charlotte and William,
So that they were quite glad he lived next door.

And he changed the spelling of his name to Mr. Great,
And often said things like "It's never too late."

"And although he didn't manage
To *catch* Santa Claus," said Charlotte one day,

"At least he *found* him."
Which is true, when you think about it, in a way,

And also he had found not only one friend
But two. Which is a pretty good place to say

THE END.

The Three Christmases

MARIAN ENGEL

Rufus and Geraldine stood staring out the window of their new house. It was eight o'clock on Christmas Eve, and snow was at last falling. The flakes were fluffy and soft against the dark night sky.

The houses across from them all looked the same. They had wide front windows, dark verandas, and high gables. Some of them had Christmas tree lights along their verandas.

Rufus and Geraldine stared at them and sighed. They had just moved into their house. They knew that the street had lots of other children on it, but they had not met any of them yet. "I wish we had lights," Geraldine said.

Rufus was thinking about something else. "What did you like best?"

"About what?"

"Daddy's apartment, silly."

"Oh." Geraldine saw herself in the white and silver place again, where everything was new, so new she was scared to touch it. "I know what you liked best."

"No you don't."

"Yes I do. It was when the waiter lit the sauce for the pancakes."

Rufus sighed and shook his head. "I'm growing out of that stuff," he said. "What I really liked was looking at all the lights. He's so high up it's like being in an airplane."

Their father had invited them to his new apartment for Christmas Eve dinner. Instead of living with them, now, he lived in a penthouse in an apartment building on the waterfront, and ordered his meals wheeled on a cart to him by a waiter in a uniform. He had treated them to a splendid supper — and delivered them home promptly because, he said, "Your baby sitter will be waiting for you."

They didn't dare tell him that there was no baby sitter, that they were going home to an empty house full of unpacked boxes, to an unmade Christmas.

What had happened was this: six months before, their parent's had had a dreadful quarrel and it was not like one of their own quarrels because it did not get made up. It ended when their father went off to get his own apartment and their mother bought this little house. The day they moved, it rained and rained. Then they found that the furnace didn't work properly, and it took days to get that fixed. They still went to their old school, but on the bus, which took a cold, long time. Their mother was proud of her own little house, but they weren't . . . much. It seemed narrow and mean to them.

Their mother was out. She had experimented with baby sitters for them, but they were experts at hassling baby sitters, and she couldn't get one any more. She had finally yelled at them, "Well, stay by yourselves, then, until I get back. I have to work for a living, and this is my busy season." She played the cello and there were a lot of concerts at Christmas time.

So they stood in their window and sighed. Their mother kept telling them everything would be all right — one day.

"I wish we had a tree," Rufus said.

"I do too," sighed Geraldine.

"I saw a guy selling trees up the street and around the corner."

"Yes, but what would we do with it? Where's the stand?"

Rufus looked despairingly at the boxes that stood around them. He knew all those boxes: he had brought them home from the supermarket himself, six a day, after school. "It might be in one of them."

"Where are the decorations?"

"In the blue suitcase, where they are every year, silly."

"But where's that, Rufus? She can never find anything."

"I saw the movers put it in the basement. Have you got any money, Geraldine?"

"Aside from Daddy's cheque I've got two dollars and forty-three cents."

"Good. I've got four-sixty. We should be able to get a tree for that: I mean, on Christmas Eve the guy wants to go home, he'll sell us one cheap. Hurry on. Get your coat."

"We're not supposed to go out again after we get home."

"She'll never know, stupid. Anyway, we're doing her a favor."

Geraldine was twelve and Rufus was eleven. She was better at rules than he was, but he was strange because wherever you set him down, he immediately learned his way around. In no time at all they were both on a corner and he was beating a man down on the price of a small Scotch pine.

Earlier in the day, it had been freezing cold. Now the soft white snow seemed to be warming the world. They carried their bargain tree down the street that was new to them. They passed strangers who said "Merry Christmas." They passed doors that were open to let visitors in.

They got to their own house. It was a job getting the tree in the door until they remembered you did it backwards, so the branches of the tree slid smoothly into the house's stomach.

Then Rufus plunged into the boxes to hunt for the tree stand, while Geraldine braved the depths of the basement to hunt for the blue suitcase. When she lugged it up the stairs, he had found the stand, his old blue quilt, all the books he wanted to read in the next ten years, and the spice rack. The living room was a mess.

They opened the ornament boxes and looked at the silver and red and blue balls that were so delicate that you could stick your fingers through them. They found the birds with spun glass tails that had been their grandmother's. The lights (but the Santa Clause bulb had gone out), the hooks, the old tinsel, the felt stockings.

It took ages to get the stand on the tree, to get the tree up and straight. They had to clear boxes away to make a place for it. They bickered about how to put up the lights, but they got them on. Rufus spent a lot of time moving bulbs around so no two of the same color would be together. Geraldine put the star on the top of the tree and made sure the glass birds had a place where they could be seen.

They stood back and looked at it. It was beautiful. It was like a sparkling necklace of city they could see from their father's balcony.

Geraldine said softly, "It makes the house feel warm."

Rufus said nothing. He began stacking boxes. He had never wanted to be neat before in his life, but he didn't want mess interfering with the view of their tree.

Geraldine let Rufus work. After all, she'd had to do a lot of picking up after him. She looked out the window and twisted her hair and wondered how she'd spend her father's cheque. He said he was giving them money so he wouldn't get in a present competition with their mother. It was a good idea. She wanted a microscope so she could see the insides of small things.

Outside the window, the street was quieter. She could see, as well as the houses across the street, the reflection of their

Christmas tree in the glass. And she noticed something else: a tiny little fir tree in their tiny little front yard, something she hadn't had time to notice before. A cold-looking sparrow was perched on top of it.

"Rufus, did you know we have a little Christmas tree of our own?"

"That thing in the front yard?"

"Yeah. Could we decorate that, do you think?"

"We don't have any outdoor lights."

But she knew what they did have, and in minutes they were popping corn and stringing cranberries. How they found the string and the darning needles that they had been looking for for days was a kind of miracle, but they did, so she strung while Rufus popped, and popped while Rufus strung, and in the end they had garlands and garlands for the birds.

And Rufus had a super idea: he also found the candles. "We can't burn the house down, can we, if they're outside?"

Geraldine glanced at the clock. It was eleven. The concert should be over. Their mother should have been home. Maybe she'd stopped off for a drink somewhere. She was kind of irresponsible. She wasn't bringing any presents, she had said. Buying them a house was all she could do. Musicians didn't make much money. "Let's go outside and do it," she said.

They put on their coats and took strings of popcorn and cranberries and a box of white candles their mother called mouse candles and matches outside. There was no way to attach the candles to the weak little branches of the silly little fir tree, so they set them in a circle around its base. There were twelve of them, and they knelt down and took turns lighting them.

Everything was very quiet. It was as if the sky was breathing snow at them. They sat on their haunches and watched the candles flicker as the snowflakes hit them. "It makes me want to sing *Silent Night*," Geraldine said, "in spite of the fact that I would never sing it at school."

"Ssh," said Rufus.

They were startled when they heard a car drive up. Their mother appeared like a ghost behind them, her arms full of parcels. Someone they didn't know took her cello into the house for her, but she stood over the little fence staring at them.

Funny: she didn't say, "You should be in bed." Later, in the kitchen, she didn't say, "How the heck did you kids manage to make such a goldurned mess?" She just stood there with a lovely smile on her face while the car drove off, and then she said, "Merry Christmas, children," and, "It's beautiful."

Finally it got cold out there and they went inside where she admired the tree. Then she wiped off the kitchen table and put her parcels down. "I guess you're too old to hang up your stockings."

"No, never!" they cried.

"Well, I'm too old . . . tonight. Did you have a good time with Daddy?"

"Yes," they said, in careful voices. They didn't want to get into a conversation about Daddy on Christmas Eve.

Neither did she. "Look, it's late," she said. "You get into your pyjamas, and I'll fill the stockings, and then you barrel down the stairs and we can pretend it's morning and open everything." It was after midnight.

Which they did. Geraldine even futilely brushed her teeth. And they brought down the things they had made for her — an ash tray in pottery class, a bookmark in sewing, a birdhouse in carpentry.

They leapt into their presents. They had not expected presents, but these were deliciously wrapped in real ribbon and fancy paper. There were boxes of tiny things wrapped to make them look bigger. "It's the year of the mortgage," she said. Staplers. Good erasers. A dozen ball-point pens for each of them. A set of Narnia books, even if they had read them before.

A really good pair of scissors for Geraldine. A vise-grip wrench for Rufus, who was always taking apart his bicycle, even in winter. Little china animals for them both.

"You'll buy your big things out of Daddy's cheque," she said. "And I do love the things you have made."

Then she sat down at the piano and played long soft music until they felt very sleepy indeed.

Outside the window, the light was changing. "Isn't it funny," Geraldine said, "the dawn is coming, and we've already had three Christmases."

Rufus yawned and counted. She was right. They had had three: their father's (and he would never forget the cart, and the pan of pancakes going up in flames, boom, like that), their mother's (Geraldine's scissors would be useful for models), and their own.

Outside, all the candles had gone out.

"Up to bed," their mother said. "We're going to Gran's tomorrow."

"Four Christmases?" Geraldine asked sleepily.

"Well," said their mother, "we've had a rough year, but there's an old expression."

"Good night, Mum," they said, "and Merry Christmas."

Never Smile Before Christmas

LESLEY CHOYCE

Sarah MacNeil wished that her mother could be happier. But there was nothing she seemed to be able to do about it. Sarah was afraid that maybe her mother was the unhappiest mother in the whole world. But when twelve-year-old Sarah woke up on a sunny summer morning in Nova Scotia, she found it hard to believe that anyone could be unhappy here.

Her bedroom looked out over a blue sparkling inlet. Sea gulls swooped up and down and a great blue heron walked gingerly through the shallows. Off towards the ocean, she could see the outline of Far Enough Island. Sarah thought that there was something magical about Far Enough Island because nobody lived there and she had never set foot on it. The island was always there in her bedroom window, full of interesting possibilities.

Jeremiah was scratching at her door. Good old Jeremiah. He was her pure black Labrador retriever, and the best friend she ever had in the world.

"Sarah, get up and let your dog out!" her mother yelled from the kitchen.

Sarah jumped up from bed and let Jeremiah into her room. Jeremiah dove at her and knocked her down on the floor, licking her nose and slobbering all over her face.

"What's going on up there?" her mother yelled again.

"Nothing," Sarah answered. Good old Jeremiah. "Dad didn't let you go on the boat again today, did he?" she said to her dog.

Jeremiah just rolled over on the floor and scratched his back by wiggling back and forth, upside down on the floor.

Sarah changed into her clothes in seconds and ran outside, with Jeremiah right on her heels. Without even saying good morning to her mother, she raced at top speed to the end of the wharf, stopping at the very last second before she would have toppled over into the icy water. Jeremiah galloped along behind her but forgot to stop at the end of the wharf. He just kept running straight out over the end, his feet kicking at the empty air. Then he splashed down hard into the water, surfaced, and turned around to swim back to the shore.

Sarah laughed and laughed. It was one of her games she liked to play with Jeremiah in the summer. He probably could have stopped if he wanted to, but Sarah knew he was a good swimmer and Jeremiah always seemed so happy after she had tricked him into flying off the end of the wharf. Now he was on the shoreline, shaking himself, water flying in a million directions.

Out past Far Enough Island, Sarah could see her dad's boat coming back from sea. That seemed strange. It was way too early for that.

Sarah walked back to the house and went into the kitchen where her mother was worrying over a pile of papers at the kitchen table. Jeremiah bounded past her and shook himself in the middle of the kitchen floor.

"Get that mangy beast out of here!" Sarah's mother went off like a canon.

"Sorry, I'll clean it up," Sarah said. The last thing she needed was to get her mother mad at her. Sarah grabbed a towel and began to mop the water drops off everything, including her mother. She grabbed poor Jeremiah by the collar and skidded him across the floor and out the door. Jeremiah looked very hurt that he was being thrown out.

"Why is Daddy headed back in so soon?" she asked her mother. She was used to her father's boat arriving back from fishing at around eleven or twelve o'clock. She saw that it was only nine-thirty.

"The fish are gone. There are hardly any left," Sarah's mother said, her voice like dry gravel.

"But there's millions of fish in the sea."

"Well, not around here, there's not. Get yourself some cereal for breakfast."

"Sure." Sarah filled a bowl to the very top.

"Sarah, that's too much. Don't waste it. Money doesn't grow on trees, you know."

Sarah poured half of it back into the box. Why didn't money grow on trees, she wondered. In fact, it should. Her parents were always worrying about money and Sarah couldn't see why. They weren't exactly poor.

Jeremiah had managed to stand up outside the door and turn the doorknob with his paw. He had it open a crack just big enough so that he could stick his nose through. He looked so funny that Sarah thought she was going to burst out laughing and spit her cereal all over the floor. Instead, she held it in. But she couldn't help having a big funny lopsided grin on her face as she tried to chew her cereal.

Her mother looked up at her. She was very annoyed about something. But it couldn't just be Sarah. Sarah was just being herself.

"Why are you smiling like that?" she asked.

Sarah shrugged her shoulders.

"Well, never smile without a good reason. You should know that. People will think there's something wrong with you. Never smile before Christmas. That's what my mother used to say." She let out a deep sigh. "And even then there's not always something to smile about."

Jeremiah had arrived in the middle of the night, six years before. It was during the worst hurricane Nova Scotia had seen in fifty years.

"What was that?" six-year-old Sarah asked. Sarah, her mother and her dad were sitting around the kitchen table. They had on a smelly kerosene lantern because the storm had knocked down a power line.

"That was just the wind," her mother said. Her mother looked frightened by the storm and her father was holding her hand.

"It'll calm down by morning," Sarah's father said, trying to be reassuring.

"What if you lose the boat?"

"I have her tied up real good. She won't go anywhere. That ole boat wouldn't know where else to go."

"Be serious," Sarah's mother said. She was staring deep into the flame.

"Stop worrying," he said.

"That's easy for you to say," Sarah's mother snapped back.

"There, I heard it again," Sarah said. "It sounded like someone crying."

"It's just your imagination," her mother explained.

"No, it wasn't," Sarah insisted. She ran to the back door and threw it open. A torrent of wind and rain blew into the room. The wind blew out the lamp and they were thrown into total darkness.

"Now what?" Sarah's mother groaned, always expecting the worst.

34

"Just be calm," her father said. "I'll find the flashlight. Sarah, close the darned door!"

The door slammed shut hard and Sarah's father fell over a chair in the dark as he tried to find the flashlight. Outside the wind howled.

Her father found the flashlight and flicked it on. There was little Sarah sitting on the wet floor by the door. In her arms was a little black puppy.

"Well, I'll be darned," her father said. "Where'd he come from?"

"I don't know, but he found us now," Sarah answered. "We're keeping him."

Her father was re-lighting the old kerosene lantern. "Well, I don't know. Your mother was never very fond of dogs. Besides, he probably belongs to someone. What do you think dear?" he asked his wife.

Sarah was so busy hugging the little squirmy puppy that she didn't even look up to see her mother crying and shaking her head up and down. "Yes," she said. "We'll keep him until we find his real home."

Now the storm had picked up even more strength. The waves pounded at the wharf. The wind tore at the wooden shingles on the roof until it had set some of them free.

"It's going to be a long night," her father said.

"This is the best night of my life," Sarah said.

No one ever lay claim to the puppy so Sarah's mother said she could keep it.

"What do you want to name him, Sarah?" she asked.

Sarah thought long and hard. "I don't know. There are so many good names. You pick one."

"I always liked the name, Jeremiah," her mother said. "I think maybe if you had a brother, I might have called him Jeremiah." Her mother looked at her with sad, gentle eyes.

"But maybe you should save that name in case I do have a brother."

"No, I don't think that will happen. I want you to use the name for the puppy."

Those were the years when the fishing was good. Sarah's dad went to sea during the good weather and nearly filled the boat with cod and hake and haddock and flounder. He sold it to the fish plant further up the inlet and came home with money in his pockets.

Her dad seemed to like getting up at five-thirty in the morning when it was still dark and going off to sea in his boat alone. "It's good to get back up the inlet before the winds come up," he'd explain. But Sarah's mother worried about him out there all alone. She always expected the worst to happen. Even in the good times.

"Stop your frettin'," he'd say. "I'm very careful." He had a big, wonderful smile on his face.

"Never smile before Christmas," his wife chided him. "You never know what can go wrong. You don't want to tempt fate with all that over-confidence."

But her dad kept smiling anyway.

Sarah didn't have many friends because she lived such a long way from town and from school. It took a half hour in their old Chevy pick-up truck to drive down the muddy gravel road to get her to school. Sarah had tried to keep track of the number of potholes.

"Three thousand and seventy five."

"What?" her mother asked.

"Three thousand and seventy five potholes to school and back."

"And next year, there'll be four thousand and seventy five," her mother answered.

Jeremiah would ride in the back of the pick-up and sniff at

the air. He looked strong and proud riding back there. And when Sarah would come home from school, they would go hiking along the beaches where Sarah would imagine them having all sorts of adventures.

Even though Jeremiah never hurt another animal, he loved to chase any living thing he came across — spruce grouse, weasels, otters, or ducks. Sarah would try to stop him, but Jeremiah just had too much wild energy that had to be released.

That was until one day when he got too close to a porcupine. Jeremiah howled with regret. He was only playing when he ran up close and nipped at the porcupine's fur which turned out not to be fur at all but hundreds of sharp needles.

Jeremiah howled in pain. Sarah ran to him and found his mouth filled with porcupine needles and blood. Sarah though Jeremiah might die. She didn't know what to do. Jeremiah didn't seem to want to follow her. He was acting crazy from the pain. Sarah tried to pick him up but he was almost as big as she was.

She heard an engine from a boat coming from the inlet and ran to the stony beach. There was her father just rounding Far Enough Island and headed home. She stood on the shore and waved and yelled for almost twenty minutes until her dad was close enough to see her. He pulled his boat in close and jumped into the shallow water.

"What is it?"

"It's Jeremiah. He chased a porcupine. Now I think he's going to die."

Sarah's father ran into the woods with her and found Jeremiah lying in a pool of blood. He wasn't moving.

Sarah's father picked him up and ran him to the boat. "Come on, honey," he said to Sarah. "We have to get the boat up the inlet to town before the tide gets too low."

On the boat, Sarah's father roared the engine and they charged towards town.

Sarah knew that her father would never take the boat up the tricky inlets unless it was a dire emergency. It was too easy to hit a rock or get stuck on a sand bar. And the boat was his life. It was what her father needed to make enough money for them to live.

"Sit up front and look for logs or rocks or shallow water," he yelled. "Just hold on good."

Sarah had to lie down on the bow of the boat with both hands braced on the wood railing. She yelled to her father to go right or left whenever she saw something ahead. The tide was dropping and the water seemed to keep getting more shallow.

Jeremiah lay very still in the back on top of the fish. He was breathing but his eyes looked funny.

"Is he going to die, Daddy?" Sarah asked.

"No," he shouted. "Just keep the look out."

Sarah knew that if they got stuck, they'd never get Jeremiah to the vet in time. She watched the water ahead very carefully, shouting when she saw a grassy shallow or a rock ahead.

At the vet's, the woman gave Jeremiah a needle. "This way he won't feel any pain," she said.

Sarah though she meant she was putting him to sleep for good. "No! You can't!" she screamed.

Her father pulled her back and the vet smiled. "No. It's not that. He's not going to die." When she pulled out the needle, she took a pair of pliers and began to gently remove the porcupine quills. Sarah counted twenty in all.

"He's a very lucky dog to have two friends like you," the vet said.

Sarah's dad had to phone her mother to come pick them up. The tide was too low to get the boat back down the inlet towards the sea, towards home.

"You could have wrecked the boat!" her mother said to them in the truck. Jeremiah was asleep across her dad's lap.

"I couldn't just let him die, could I?" her father said. He seemed really mad at her for saying it. Sarah just remained quiet.

"Well, it's just an old dog," her mother said. "If you wrecked the boat, then what would we do for money?"

"It's not just an old dog," Sarah said, angry now at what her mother said. She didn't understand at all.

Her mother stopped the truck and slapped her across the face. Sarah felt it like a hot burn across her cheek. Sarah raised her arm to hit her mother back but her father grabbed onto her wrist, firm but gently.

"You shouldn't have slapped her," he said.

Sarah's mother turned off the truck. She threw the keys at Sarah's father. Then she got out, slammed the door, and began walking.

"I'm walking home. You drive home just the two of you. I'm the only one who does all the worrying around here. Get on with you."

Sarah's father tried to stop her but it did no good. He lay Jeremiah on the seat and slid over to drive.

"Why is she like that?" Sarah asked.

"It's hard to explain," her father said. "Her mother was very cruel to her. And I think she always hoped I'd be something more than a fisherman."

"What's wrong with being a fisherman?"

"Well, sometimes you have good times and sometimes you have bad times. And you know her father drowned."

"Yeh, but you can swim."

"Sure, I can swim good," he said, even though it was a lie but it was one he had repeated over and over so many times that he half believed it.

Sarah's father couldn't get out to sea the next day to fish because his boat was tied up in town and he had missed the high tide in the middle of the night. So he lost a day's fishing which cost the family needed money.

Just like Sarah's mother had predicted, things did get worse. It seemed that every year there were fewer and fewer fish. The weather was getting stormier and colder early in the fall. With less fish and fewer days in the season, the fish plant closed down and there was no place to sell what little catch there was. Her father lost his boat to the bank because he couldn't keep up payments. He took a job at a garage in town fixing cars but he hated it.

"At least it's money coming in," his mother would say. "But I know it's gonna get worse before it gets better. If it ever gets better."

Sarah didn't like school very much, and now that her father was working in town, she had to hang around the gas station until five o'clock when he got off work so he could drive her home.

She missed her long walks along the beach with Jeremiah in the afternoons. She hated the garage which always smelled of cigarettes and grease and gasoline. Men and boys stood around and talked tough. Her father was always telling them to use good language when Sarah was around but it didn't do any good.

And she really missed waking up in the morning and seeing her father's boat way off out to sea towards Far Enough Island. She missed how happy her father had been coming home to the wharf with a boatload of fish.

"Since you're not fishing any more, we might as well sell the place and move to town. It would be better for Sarah and it would be better for us," her mother said in a sour voice.

"Jeremiah would hate it in town," Sarah said.

"Then we'd just have to find Jeremiah a new home. He costs us an arm and a leg to feed anyway. And we need to save all the money we can. Hard times might be ahead."

Sarah's father looked down at the floor and didn't say a thing. But the next day when he took Sarah to town, he said he didn't want her to go to school, that he needed her help. First they went to the bank and he took out almost all their saved money. Then they drove over to Old Man Fogerty's little run-down wharf on a narrow channel of the inlet.

Old Man Fogerty was eighty-five-years old. "She's a good boat," he said. "Old but good. You treat her well, she'll last you a few years."

The boat was certainly old. But it didn't look so good.

"All it needs is a little paint," her father said. "With a little luck I'll be able to afford better in a couple of years."

Her father handed over the money.

"You bought it? What will mother say?" Sarah asked.

"I don't know. I just know I'm fed up with the garage and I don't want to move to town. Now lie down up front there and help me steer out the channel to home before the tide slips."

So Sarah helped steer her dad and his new boat home.

The engine made loud coughing noises. It sputtered and stalled several times but eventually they made it. When they pulled up, there was Sarah's mother on the wharf with her arms folded and a dirty look on her face. When Jeremiah spotted them he came racing down the boards and launched himself out off the wharf before her mother could stop him. He jumped halfway to the boat before splashing down and swimming the rest of the way. Sarah's dad helped him up over the side and as Jeremiah shook the water off, he sprayed Sarah and her dad until they were soaked.

It should have been a very funny scene. But Sarah's mother wasn't laughing at all.

Sarah's father worked night and day at fixing up the boat.

"It too old," Sarah's mother said.

"Fogerty says there's life in her yet."

"I don't trust you out there alone in that old boat. Something could happen."

"Why don't you take Jeremiah along," Sarah said. "Just for company."

"He'd only get in the way," her father said. "A dog's not much good on a boat."

"But he likes the water."

Sarah's mother scowled. "Yes, why not take the dog with you. Get him out from being underfoot."

Sarah's father nodded okay. He didn't mind having a little dog company on board if it gave his wife one less thing to complain about.

It was getting late in the year for a good start but the fish had come back now and there was plenty to catch.

Sarah was in school when her father came back each day with the boat, but she knew things were going well.

She missed Jeremiah jumping up and licking her in the face every morning but she did get to play with him after school. And she liked the idea of good old Jeremiah being out there with her father every day, out beyond Far Enough Island. The only problem was that Jeremiah now always smelled like fish and he wasn't allowed into the house anymore, except when Sarah sneaked him in when her mother wasn't home.

"I knew everything would work out," her father told the family one night at dinner. "I got the boat. The cod are back. I'm even getting a pretty good price from the new buyer. I'll have a newer boat soon."

"I think it's Jeremiah on the boat that brings good luck," Sarah said. Sarah and her father looked at each other and beamed.

Sarah's mother wasn't convinced. "It's always calmest just before the storm," she said. "Season's not over yet. Just wait. Never smile before Christmas, that's what I'd say."

But things were going well. And everyone should have been happy, only Sarah's mother couldn't convince herself things were going to be all right.

Then one morning that started out bright and cheery, the wind switched and a heavy fog pulled up the inlet.

It was a Saturday and Sarah was not in school. Her mother stared out the window and began to wring her hands together. "I hope he gets back in here soon."

"He'll be okay. He knows the inlet out there. Don't worry," Sarah said.

But she worried.

Her father might have high-tailed it shoreward before the fog if he wasn't having trouble with the engine. But the old contraption was giving him problems. Water in the carburettor. He was stalled and drifting, still trying to fix it, when the fog pulled in tight so that he couldn't see a thing. Then the wind stopped and it was dead still.

Jeremiah was nervous, nosing around the boat, wondering why it was quiet and they weren't moving.

Sarah's father had the lid off the engine and was pouring gasoline down the carburettor. He tried the ignition. It backfired a couple of times. Then suddenly it coughed a long flame out the mouth of the carburettor, knocking her father off balance and back onto the slimy pile of the day's catch. Before he could turn off the ignition, gasoline was leaking out of the fuel line and the flame had caught it on fire.

Sarah's father grabbed a heavy tarp and threw it across the engine. But it too caught fire. Jeremiah was barking loud and fiercely as if the fire was a living thing and he was going to fend it off.

The fire began to creep out onto the floorboards. It was headed towards the gas tank. Sarah's father tried to sneak past it towards the small cabin to grab for a life vest, but a new, more violent burst of flame roared up from below the deck, knocking him overboard. In the water, he flailed his arms. He kept telling himself that he did know how to swim. He had told that to his wife so often that he truly believed it. The water was cold. It was like sharp knives sticking into his arms and legs.

On the boat, Jeremiah continued to bark. What should he do, Sarah's father wondered. Should he get back in the boat or try to swim away from it? He tried to stay calm, kept himself floating, and tried to think it through.

"Here. Jeremiah. Jump!" He yelled.

Jeremiah launched into the water and swam towards him.

Now the entire boat was aflame. Within minutes it would be down. There was no explosion, just the crackle of wood.

All too soon, the water was up to the gunwales and the flame diminished to nothing as the boat sank beneath. Still hanging onto Jeremiah to keep him afloat, Sarah's father swam back towards where the boat had gone down, hoping to find a plank, some sort of wood to hold onto and keep him up. He found a section of the hull that had been left floating. It wasn't much but it was enough to keep his head above water. Around them was a sickly pool of oil and gas and black ash. The fog was now so dense he couldn't see more than ten feet in any direction. Jeremiah pulled himself up onto a section of deck that was afloat. At first he began to whine. But then he shook himself and began to bark loudly.

"I'm sorry old boy," Sarah's father said. "I don't know what good barking will do you. You might as well save your breath."

But Jeremiah went on barking louder and louder. It was like he had gone crazy and couldn't stop himself.

Sarah's father felt so cold and weak from being in the water that he grew discouraged. He could think of no plan of action. He felt helpless and doomed. The dog barked on and he wished he could make Jeremiah shut up.

After what seemed to be an hour, he thought he heard a boat engine. It was far off in the fog but coming closer.

"Keep barking!" he now shouted to Jeremiah, but Jeremiah was floating away from him.

The boat was coming closer. Sarah's father convinced himself he had to move. He let go of the wood and began to swim towards the engine noise. Then he heard Jeremiah splash into the water and swim up to him. "Over here!" he yelled. But as he did so, his mouth filled with water. He felt himself sink under. He reached out with his hands and there was Jeremiah. He grabbed the collar, pulled the dog under with him, but Jeremiah kicked his legs and kept swimming.

The boat was nearly on top of them.

"Cut the engine quick," someone shouted. Arms were reaching down. Sarah's father was fighting to stay above water. He knew he was pushing down on Jeremiah. It was the only thing keeping him from sinking altogether. He knew he was probably drowning the dog. But he couldn't help it.

Then the arms had grabbed him. He was being hauled up into a boat. He was flat on the deck and his lungs were heaving. He was gasping for air.

"Anyone else out here?" a man's voice asked frantically.

"A dog," Sarah's father said. "Jeremiah. Did you get the dog?"

"I didn't see no dog but that's why I came this way. I heard some fool dog barking his head off. But if he was out there he's not around now," the man said.

Sarah's father pulled himself up to the gunwale and looked over the side. There was nothing to see. No Jeremiah, nothing but a thick ugly fog.

They circled around for twenty minutes but saw and heard nothing.

"He saved my life," Sarah's father said and sunk back onto the floor.

"I told you things would get worse. I felt it in my bones. We're just a family of bad luck."

"That's not true," Sarah shouted back at her mother. "If it wasn't for Jeremiah, Dad would be dead by now."

Her dad hung his head down. "That's right. I have to go look for him. I'll get Hopper to loan me his boat."

"Not in this weather, you're not!" Sarah's mother insisted.

"I suppose you're right. One swim in the sink is one too many."

"But we need to look for him!" Sarah screamed. "He might be alive."

"He couldn't swim all the way back here," her father said.

"But he might have made it to the island. He could have, you know?"

Her father shook his head. "It's unlikely. I don't know how close to the island we were. Besides, how could he find it in all that fog?"

"He's just dead and that's all there is to it," her mother said. "Now let's just leave it at that."

But by morning the sun was out. "I'm going looking for him. Hopper said I could borrow his boat." Sarah's father had a life jacket on. Just then Sarah burst out of her room. She had one on as well. "I'm going too," she announced.

Her father put an arm around her and gave her a hug. "Sure. We'll both look for him."

Her mother looked furious. "Sure, get both of you drowned now! That's all I need."

Sarah's father walked up to her and took her by the shoulders, kissed her on the cheek, and whispered something in her ear. "Please, we'll be careful," Sarah said. "We won't go past the island. We just have to look once."

They were gone most of the day. Sarah and her father walked all around the island and looked everywhere along the beaches. But there was no sign of Jeremiah.

"I'm sorry, honey," her father said.

Sarah tried not to cry but she couldn't help it. "He was my only real friend," she said, and the tears kept coming all the way home. But when she entered the kitchen and saw how happy her mother was to have the two of them home safe, she brightened a little.

They had a big dinner without any arguing at all, and her father promised to try to get his job back at the garage.

After that the weather turned very cold for so early in the year. All the fishermen pulled up their boats weeks before they normally would. Raging northeast storms pummelled the coast. Then came snow in October. Sleet and ice and snow. Schools were closed. Sarah's father got fired from his garage job and went on unemployment.

Sarah's mother always wore a frown on her face. "We should have just packed up and moved long ago. Now's the time. Let's get away from here."

But Sarah didn't want to move. She kept remembering those happy sunny days walking the shoreline with Jeremiah and discovering all sorts of things. She still couldn't believe he was gone. Some mornings she'd wake up and expect him to come bounding into her room, smelling of fish and mud. But she kept reminding herself that if it wasn't for Jeremiah, she wouldn't have a father.

It was Christmas morning and things had been so rotten around Sarah's house for so long that she knew even today was going to be rotten.

The only thing that would make it better was a miracle. Her parents argued all the time about money and about moving. Sarah, herself, would get so tired of it all that she'd just scream,

47

"Shut up!" and run out of the living room and lock herself in her bedroom.

It had been a strange December. The harbor froze up early and the ice grew thick across the shallows and even out into the channel.

"It's a sign of worse things to come," her mother said. "I've never seen anything like it."

They could no longer afford oil for the furnace so her father spent much of his time each day cutting spruce logs and hauling them home for firewood, splitting them and stoking the stoves.

The ice had crept all the way out the inlet almost to Far Enough Island. It was the first time that had happened this early, Old Man Fogerty said, since 1915. It was going to be a long, cold, sad winter.

"But today is Christmas," her mother said. "And I'm not going to worry about a thing. Today I want all of us to be happy!"

She wasn't very convincing but she tried. She had always said it was the one day that she refused to worry about anything. She woke Sarah early in the morning, even before the sun was up, with a peck on the cheek.

"Merry Christmas, Sarah."

But Sarah woke up thinking about Jeremiah and all the other Christmases he had been there. She remembered how he had torn up the wrapping paper to get at his presents — dog bones and leather chew toys. He had been so funny and so cute. And now she would never, ever see him again.

Her mother tried singing to Sarah to cheer her up but it didn't do any good.

The presents were opened and Sarah tried to act surprised and happy but nothing there interested her.

Her father tried to be cheerful but he was a lousy faker.

By the end of the day, her mother's good humor had worn off and they all sat around tired and depressed.

"This is the worst Christmas of my life," Sarah finally said out loud. "I never want to have another Christmas as long as I live." She sulked off to her room, slammed her door, and went to bed.

The day after Christmas was something else. The ice storm had stopped. The sun was shining brightly and Sarah flipped open the shade on her window. All the trees were coated in ice and the inlet was like one sheet of pure, clear glass. The wharf was like some magical creation coated in crystal. And off in the distance, Far Enough Island, with all the trees glazed with ice, appeared like a magical kingdom.

Sarah just wanted to keep looking out her window. She didn't want to go down to her family and face all the gloom and worry. If only she could just stare out her window like this forever and see the world as a gleaming magical place, everything would be all right.

And then, off in the far distance, she saw a small black speck that arrested her attention. Out towards Far Enough Island something was moving on the ice. An otter, she decided. She should get her father's binoculars and watch him.

She quietly slipped out of her bed and into her parents' bedroom. They were still asleep. But by the window were the binoculars. She returned with them to her room.

At first she couldn't relocate the animal in the glare of ice. But then she found it. Maybe it wasn't an otter, after all. It was larger than an otter, for sure. And it had longer legs. It was running. Running towards her.

Her eyes began to tear up. She couldn't focus properly. She wiped her face. Yes, whatever it was, it was running. And it was black. It kept slipping and falling on the ice. But it was running towards her from the island. She closed her eyes and pinched herself to make sure she was awake. She had had dreams like this before. And always when she opened her eyes, she was alone, and the image was gone.

She re-opened her eyes. The pinch had hurt. She was awake. She put the binoculars to her eyes again.

It was him. The ice now stretched from Far Enough Island all the way to her shore. He was on his way home.

Sarah ran downstairs and on outside into the bright cold air. She yelled "Jeremiah!" out across the vast expanse of ice.

Then she heard the first bark. It was his unmistakeable bark. She started to run towards him, out across the frozen yard, but she slipped and fell. Everything was covered with ice and it was almost impossible to take a step.

Her shout had awakened her father and mother. They were there beside her now, her father helping her up.

"He was there after all," her father said, his eyes fixed on the black animal still making his difficult way across the ice. "He had made it to the island and he was too tired or injured for us to find him. And now that the inlet has froze up all the way to the island, he's coming back."

"Today is the day for all of us to smile," Sarah's mother said.

All three of them, still in their night clothes, began a slow slippery walk across the icy yard towards the inlet, towards Jeremiah. Sarah wanted to run, but her parents held her back. When they reached the wharf, there was Jeremiah, his feet going every which way as he scratched the ice to make his way home.

Sarah knelt down on the cold glassy surface and felt the hot, familiar breath of Jeremiah. She let him lick her face and bark loud as a canon shot right in her ear.

With a lot of slipping and sliding, they all found their way back into the warm kitchen where Jeremiah was treated to all the leftover Christmas dinner he wanted.

And as soon as Sarah had calmed down enough to allow her brain half a chance to think, she realized by looking at her mother and her father and at Jeremiah that things were going to get better after this. It wouldn't matter if the fish never came back or if the money was tight or if the whole world froze solid. There would always be this moment that would make every one of them smile, any time of the year, long before Christmas.

The Christmas Log

MARY ALICE DOWNIE

"Once upon a time, my children . . ." the grandmother began.

At this moment there was a stir among the listeners in the farmhouse kitchen. Everyone moved in his place. The father coughed; the little ones leaned forward with elbows on knees and chins in hands.

"Once upon a time, my children," repeated the grandmother. "There was an old château, very old indeed, very gloomy and solitary. It stood on the rocky flank of a hill crowned by a forest of giant oaks. Its real name was the castle of Kerfoël but it was better known as the Devil's Tower. It was said that in the old days the Devil had built a forge and furnace in the highest room of the turret. There he made gold for the lords of the domain. They in turn belonged to him from generation to generation.

There must have been an evil source for their wealth. From the top of that gloomy tower one could see nothing but barren moors, with here and there a menhir. These big fairy-stones that stand up like men are called Satan's distaffs.

I must tell you, my children, that this story took place in France in the old province of Brittany, where *my* grandmother came from when our people settled in this land of Canada.

At the time of my story, the lord of Kerfoël and owner of the Devil's Tower was named Robert. He had been crippled from birth and was bandy-legged and club-footed as well, but he was still as strong as a giant. He had an evil reputation, for apart from his deformity, he was both ill-tempered and wicked. He hunted wild boar in the woods, even on Sundays. He harried the peasants, blasphemed the name of God, and was never seen in church. He ate meat on Fridays and he laughed at funerals.

People whispered that they had seen him far away on the moors at night, limping along on his twisted leg in company with the menhirs. They said that these stones followed him as obediently as dogs in the moonlight. No one knew where he was going. In short, the Count Robert de Kerfoël was a wretched sinner who feared neither God nor Satan.

His mother had died of a broken heart because of his sinful ways. His father had died without confession in a corner of the forest where his body had been found half-devoured by wolves. The son was to finish more miserably still."

Not a finger moved; every word, every syllable was snapped up as the grandmother continued her story.

"You have seen the man in the moon, haven't you, my children?"

"Yes, Me'mère."

"A lame man."

"Who is going down hill."

"With a bundle of straw on his shoulders."

"No, a faggot."

"A log, little ones, a burning log. You can see him at night when the stars glitter in the sky and there is a full moon. He is especially clear on Christmas night when the rosy light from the church windows mingles with the pale radiance that falls from Heaven on the snow-covered hills. You have seen him, haven't you?"

"Yes, yes, Me'mère."

"With the log on his shoulder."

"Yes, and with his crooked leg."

"Well, listen now. In Brittany, the valiant land of Brittany, they did not celebrate Christmas as we do here with midnight mass and afterwards a glass of liquor and a branch of croquignole sprinkled with powdered sugar. There it was the peasants' day, the feast of the poor and the country festival above all others. The folk gathered in the châteaux and farmhouses and waited, young and old, with all manner of rejoicing, for midnight mass.

First they had the *Christmas log*. It was dragged into the hall, baptized with a glass of wine from the last vintage and burnt in the great chimney place. After that they sang the old carols and feasted with cider and crusty little cakes called 'nieulles.'

Then they danced. How they danced! Not waltzes or quadrilles or cotillions as they do in the Governor's mansion in Quebec. In Brittany the boys and girls danced the bourrèe and the cariole to the sound of the binioux, which is something like the bagpipes that the Scotch play in their misty hills.

As you can easily imagine, my pets, Christmas was not celebrated in this way at the Devil's Tower. The people at the château on that night went to church and then returned to gather silently around the hearth. The old game-keeper Le Goffic would tell a tale or sing an old carol in a very low voice for fear of being overheard by the master. Season after season went by in sadness and fear without a moment's gaiety or joy.

One morning it happened that Count Robert sent for his steward Yvon Kerouak and they had a long talk. Then he ordered his best horse saddled. He set off without saying a word to a living soul. Where did he go? No one knew.

Months followed weeks and years months. There was no

news of him. People supposed him dead and made the sign of the cross when they heard the name of the Count de Kerfoël. He must have been the victim of some dreadful punishment. He would surely never be seen again in this life, or if it pleased God, in the other either.

Twenty years went by. The steward, the housekeeper and the other servants had grown grey. Old Le Goffic counted over eighty years.

Everyone was convinced that Count Robert would never return. The inhabitants of the old château began to lead a quieter life and merry times were as frequent at the Devil's Tower as anywhere else.

Christmas Eve was a special time of gaiety and feasting under the battlements of the old tower. One year the inhabitants of the château decided to celebrate with exceptional splendor. A huge log was cut from one of the giant oaks in the park and prepared for the ceremony. At eight o'clock that night, all the neighbors, the binioux-player in the lead, crowded into the great hall of the château. It was illuminated by pine-branches and the lively blaze of the Christmas log itself in the hearth.

The merrymakers shouted with laughter. Their goblets rang as they toasted each other and then swallowed the foaming cider, while the long snuffling notes of the binoux droned on.

Suddenly: "Noël! Noël!" they all cried so loudly that the leaded panes of the old Gothic windows tinkled in response. The Christmas log caught fire. It crackled and spread showers of sparks.

"The baptism! The baptism!" they cried.

"Uncle le Goffic! To you the honors of the ceremony."

"Come, baptize the Christmas log, Uncle le Goffic."

"Uncle le Goffic! Uncle le Goffic!"

Then all fell on their knees, while the old game-keeper, bare-headed, advanced towards the fireplace. The light shone like a glory around his long white hair.

"In the name of the Father and of the Son and of the Holy Ghost," he said. His knotted trembling hand dropped the wine like a string of rubies on the massive log.

Before they could answer "amen" a wild gust of wind swept aside the flames on the hearth. There in the open doorway stood the squat figure of Count Robert de Kerfoël!

The people stood, dumb and horrified. Count Robert glanced about ferociously and advanced with drawn sword through the terrified peasants.

"Par la mort Dieux! How long has my château been the scene of such mummeries!" He turned to his old groom and pointed to the blazing fire. "Joel! Remove this emblem of a cursed superstition."

Despite their fear, the peasants cried aloud.

"The Christmas log?"

"Yes, the Christmas log. Out with it! Do you hear me, Joel?"

"My Lord Count," Joel replied, kneeling in terror. "The Christmas log is sacred. I would die rather than touch it."

"By all the devils!" screamed the count, half-maddened with rage. "Who commands here?"

"My Lord Count," said the steward. "The Christmas log is hallowed. It would be a sin to touch it."

"It would be a sin," repeated the others like an echo.

"Stupid idiots!" cried Count Robert. He seized two jugs of cider and emptied them over the burning log. With his own hands he pulled it from the fireplace and heaved it onto his shoulder. He paid no attention to the fire-brands that singed his hair and shrivelled his skin.

"My Lord Count," warned the old game-keeper, shivering from head to foot. "The Christmas log has been baptized. Beware of God's hand, my Lord Count!"

"Sacrilege!" cried several among the crowd. The Count, limping dreadfully, staggered across the threshold. His back was bent under the weight of the smoking log. He disappeared into the darkness outside, blaspheming horribly.

"Let us kneel and pray!" cried old le Goffic.

Too late. An inhuman cry sounded in the night. Count Robert de Kerfoël, last Lord of the Devil's Tower, was never seen again.

Ever since that night, my children, in clear weather, on the shining disk of the moon you can see a man with a twisted knee. He stoops under a strange burden and those who see well enough say that it is a half-burnt log still flaming here and there. The unfortunate Count Robert is condemned to carry that heavy burden on his shoulder until the day of the last judgment.

(Retold from *Christmas in French Canada* by Louis Frèchette, 1899)

Christmas Under a
Pale Green Sky

BARBARA NOVAK

Santa Claus
North Pole, Planet Earth

December 1, 2054

Dear Santa,
   Thanks for the laser camera you gave me last Christmas. It takes good 3-D pictures.
   What I would like this year is some hockey equipment, especially skates and a hockey stick, more if possible.
   The problem is nobody will be home at my house. We won't even be on Earth. My parents have to go to Borp for an intergalactic travel conference so they're taking my sister and me with them. We'll be staying at the Borp Holiday Inn Bubble Complex. It's supposed to be a nice place if you like to eat slow food which I don't. I only like fast food. But my dad says I have to go. Do you know what it's like on Borp? There is no snow, no ice, and no Christmas. Just food.

Yours truly,

Fenwick Lovington

"You've wasted your time, borple brain," said Trillium when she finished reading the copy Fenwick had stored on his computer. "Santa Claus has enough trouble getting around to all the girls and boys on Earth. He won't come all the way to Borp. It's not even in the Milky Way."

"He will, too!" Fenwick shut off his computer with an angry jab of his forefinger. The screen went dark. He didn't know which was worse: being on Borp for Christmas, or sharing a hotel room with his sister.

She leaned across the king-size bed and poked him in the ribs. "Besides, who plays hockey? It's an *archaic* sport! Why didn't you ask Santa for the video game?"

"Because I like the real thing." Every since seeing some old cassettes of a guy named Gretzky play for the Edmonton Oilers way back in the 1980s, Fenwick had dreamed of being a hockey star when he grew up.

His sister snorted. "You can't even *walk* without tripping over your feet."

Fenwick thought longingly of his own bed in his own room in his own home on his own planet and felt tears sting his eyes. Tonight was Christmas Eve. What if Trillium was right? It was a long way to expect Santa to come, especially by sled.

Going over to the window, he leaned against the sill and looked over past the bubble to Borp proper, where the sun rarely set in the pale green sky. He could see that it was a pretty planet; it was just that he missed Earth. Directly below, three storeys down, a marble fountain sprayed thin jets of water almost as high as the window.

He swallowed hard, not wanting Trillium to see him cry. She was eleven. Once he'd believed he could catch up to her, but now he knew that no matter how old he was he'd always be three years younger than Trillium.

"Didn't *you* ask Santa for anything?"

"Peace and goodwill among all creatures in the universe,"

she replied sweetly.

"Ha!"

"And a new video-phone," she added. "And some neon barrettes for my hair, and a subscription to *Seventeen* magazine."

Fenwick whirled around "There! You see? Why would you have bothered asking Santa for anything if you didn't think he'd bring it to Borp?"

Trillium sighed impatiently. "I didn't ask him to bring it *here*. I explained that no one would be home and asked him to leave the stuff in the living room. And I left some cookies for him in the dispenser."

Fenwick wished he'd thought of that.

Just then there was a knock at their door. It was their parents, stopping by on their way to the convention.

"There's a party downstairs for the children who are staying at the hotel to meet some children from Borp," their mother told them.

"Some Eaties are there?" Trillium shrieked. "Oh, they're so cute!"

Fenwick groaned. The preparation and consuming of food was of such importance on Borp that its inhabitants were called Eaties.

"What should I wear?" asked Trillium. "Is there dancing?"

"No, but there's some good food," said their father.

Fenwick perked up. "Fast food?"

His mother shook her head. "But try some, dear. You might like it. It's very wholesome. In the olden days, before Mac-Donalds, that's what we humans used to eat all the time."

Fenwick sighed. He knew all that. He knew about stoves and refrigerators and the preparation and cooking of food. He'd studied it on his computer and found the whole subject faintly disgusting. He would have given anything right then for a couple of Christmas turkeyburgers from the food dispenser in their own kitchen.

His father placed a hand on Fenwick's shoulder. "I know this isn't how you'd like to spend Christmas," he said. "But if we refused to come to this convention then your mother and I would lose our jobs."

Fenwick nodded.

"The meeting will be over early," he continued. "We'll pick you up at the party as soon as we can so that we can all spend Christmas Eve together."

Their watches signaled the hour.

"We have to dash," said their mother, kissing the children good-bye.

"I'm not going," Fenwick announced as soon as their parents had left.

"You have to go," said Trillium.

"Why?"

"Because I'm going and I'm older and I'm supposed to be responsible for you."

"Goodbye," Fenwick said firmly. "Have fun."

"Fine. If you stay, I'll stay." Trillium strode across the room to their luggage and picked up her violin case. "You don't mind if I practice my violin for a few hours, do you?"

Seconds later the room was filled with the most terrible screeches and squawks.

"Stop!" Fenwick begged, his hands over his ears. "I'll go!"

He brightened when he saw the lobby glittering with Christmas decorations. A big plastic pine tree stood in one corner with a bright silver star sparkling at the top and a pile of colorful packages underneath.

"But I thought they didn't have Christmas on Borp," he said.

"This is an Earth hotel," Trillium reminded him just as a chorus of *O Come, All Ye Faithful* came blaring over the sound system.

"Look!" she cried, pointing to a jolly fat man with a white

beard and a red suit who was ho-hoing his way in their direction, a big sack over his shoulder.

Fenwick's heart beat faster.

"Ho! Ho! Ho! And a Hairy Mismuch to you!"

His heart sank as he recognized the hollow-sounding voice of a computerized robot. Still, an electronic Santa was better than no Santa at all, and this one was offering him a candy cane.

As Fenwick reached out to take it, the Santa Claus robot cried, "Hairy Mismuch! Hairy Mismuch!" and plunged the candy into his own ear. "Ho! Ho! Ho!"

Trillium burst out laughing. Fenwick grumbled, "Someone better re-program that robot or it's going to cause serious damage."

Fenwick's chin rested glumly in his hand. His elbow was propped on the table at which he sat alone in the corner of the room, looking around at the party. There was Trillium, busy braiding an Eatie girl's tentacles. Fenwick couldn't understand why everyone kept saying the Eaties were so cute. He thought they looked very peculiar with their glowing green skin (a sign of health in Borp), and their big eyes and pointy ears and extendable limbs. One was approaching him now, a plate of food in his rubbery hands.

"Bxvd zp ni qxprbu gggs pt, Borp?"

Fenwick quickly adjusted his automatic translator. "I beg your pardon?"

"Would you care for a fresh mushroom lovingly stuffed with Borp cheese?" asked the Eatie.

"No, thank you." But Fenwick quickly changed his mind when he saw the Eatie turn pale and begin to shrivel. He remembered how sensitive they were. And of course, it was a terrible insult to refuse food on Borp. "I'd love one," he said, and was relieved to see the Eatie recover immediately.

He popped it into his mouth and swallowed fast, so he

wouldn't have to taste it.

"Another?" asked the Eatie.

Fenwick ate this one slowly, nibbling discreetly around the edges.

"I don't suppose you have Christmas pudding pops here, do you?"

"Pops?" The Eatie shook his head. "Does not compute."

"No, I didn't think so."

"But I know all about Christmas," the Eatie said. "I did a project on it for planetary studies at school."

Fenwick had heard about schools from his grandfather, and he'd visited a model classroom in a museum once. In some ways the Eaties were very old-fashioned. If they still had schools, he thought, maybe they played hockey. "Do you have hockey here?" he asked.

"Hockey? What does it taste like?"

Fenwick shook his head. "It's a game."

"A game! Like hot potato?"

"Not exactly," said Fenwick.

"Butter the muffin?"

"Do all your games have something to do with food?"

The Eatie nodded.

Fenwick began to explain to him about hockey. To his surprise, his new friend seemed very interested. He wanted to know where he could get some skates.

Before Fenwick could reply they were interrupted by the sound of an explosion in the lobby. Startled, they leaped to their feet and rushed out.

There, in a crumpled heap in front of a roaring fire in the fireplace, lay what remained of the Santa Claus robot. Wisps of smoke curled up like angel hair from the exposed wires, filling the lobby with the sharp odor of melted plastic.

Their feet crunched over broken candy canes as Fenwick and the Eatie pushed past the crowd of people and saw a man doubled over in pain near the robot, his face hidden in his hands.

"That's my dad!" cried Fenwick.

His mother looked up from where she knelt beside the groaning father. Fenwick ran into her arms.

The wail of a siren grew louder as an ambulance pulled up outside.

Fenwick, Trillium, and the Eatie sat quietly in the small waiting room of the bubble complex hospital while Mrs. Lovington described what had happened.

They had been on their way to meet the children when Mr. Lovington noticed the Santa Claus robot under the Christmas tree in the lobby stuffing the gifts into his sack. They thought it was strange, especially since those presents had been provided by the guests for their children. Mrs. Lovington wondered whether the Santa was preparing to hand them out personally. Then her husband pointed to the broken candy canes strewn all over the carpet. It seemed very suspicious indeed. In the meantime, the Santa began marching across the lobby towards the fireplace.

"Stop!" Mr. Lovington cried.

The Santa marched even faster. Mr. Lovington ran after him. The Santa swung his sack around and bashed Mr. Lovington in the nose. As he fell, he grabbed one of the Santa's boots, causing the robot to crash down to the floor where it exploded. But not before the sack went flying into the fire.

"Your father is a very brave man," said the hotel manager, who had arrived while Mrs. Lovington was telling the story. "We're terribly sorry. We suspect it was a loose connection or a defective microchip. It's being checked out now."

"When can we see Dad?" Fenwick asked.

"You can see him now," said the doctor as he came into the waiting room. "It looks worse than it is. Fortunately, the only thing broken is his nose."

When Fenwick and Trillium saw their father lying under the white hospital sheet, his eyes ringed with ugly bruises, his face swollen and his nose covered with tape, they burst into tears.

"What an awful Christmas this is turning out to be for you," their father murmured. "I'm sorry about the presents."

"You could have been killed!" sobbed Fenwick.

Trillium sniffed. "We don't care about the presents."

"No!" Fenwick shook his head.

"Still," their father replied, taking their hands in his, "it's not a very nice way to spend Christmas, sitting around a hospital room in Borp."

"I have good news," said the doctor. "I've signed your release papers. You can all go back to the hotel."

The manager offered to have Christmas dinner sent up to their rooms, on the house.

The Lovington family looked at each other sadly. They all wished they were back on earth.

"I have an idea," said the Eatie. "Will you excuse me? I want to phone home."

"What did he say?" asked Mr. Lovington, who wasn't wearing his automatic translator.

"The Eatie's phoning home," Fenwick explained.

A moment later he returned. "It's all settled. You're invited to spend Christmas Eve at my house."

"Can we, Dad?" Fenwick asked, his eyes sparkling.

His father smiled. "I don't know. We'll have to wear space helmets outside the bubble, and I don't think mine will fit until this swelling goes down."

The hotel manager insisted on providing the whole family with expensive atmosphere adaptors so none of them would have to wear space helmets. And he offered them transportation as well.

"Then it's all settled," Mr. Lovington said, looking very pleased.

None of them had ever been to an Eatie home before. While still outside, Fenwick could smell a wonderful aroma, similar to that of turkeyburgers but much richer.

The Eatie's parents greeted them at the door. Introductions were made and they were led into the living room. There, they gasped in astonishment. In the corner next to the window stood a beautiful Christmas tree sparkling with colorful lights and tinsel. Strings of popcorn and candy canes and gingerbread men hung on every branch. On the top perched an angel holding a silver star. Underneath the tree was a small pile of hay in which a doll lay, its eyes closed. Kneeling in front of it were the clay figures of Joseph and Mary.

"It's my project," said the Eatie. "For school, remember?"

Fenwick nodded, too overwhelmed to speak.

"I hope you got an A," said Trillium shyly.

The Eatie's eyes shone. "Is it accurate?"

"A real, old-fashioned Christmas!" exclaimed Mrs. Lovington, fingering one of the pine needles. "Look, children! A real tree!"

When Fenwick recovered his voice, he asked, "What's that delicious smell?"

"The rest of my project," said his friend, leading everyone into the kitchen, where the aroma was even stronger. They sat down to the best Christmas dinner any of them had ever tasted: roast turkey with stuffing and gravy, and roast potatoes and fresh cranberry sauce, glazed carrots, home-made sourdough bread with sweet, hand-churned butter, crisp salad, and hot Christmas pudding and mince-meat pies and shortbread cookies for dessert.

"I can't believe this is *slow food*," Fenwick said, helping himself to more turkey.

"I hope I'm not being rude," said Trillium, "but why are those socks hanging over the oven door?"

The Eaties laughed. "Because we don't have a fireplace!"

When Fenwick opened his eyes in the hotel room the next morning the first thing he saw was a shiny new pair of skates and a hockey stick beside his bed.

Trillium was already up. She was sitting in the arm-chair next to the window flipping through a *Seventeen* magazine. A new pair of neon barrettes held back her hair. Beside her, on the table, sat her new video-phone.

"He came!" Fenwick cried. "Santa was here!"

Trillium grinned at him. "Have a look out the window."

Fenwick jumped out of bed and ran across the room. He looked outside and saw that the fountain had disappeared. In its place was a hockey rink enclosed in a clear plastic bubble of its own. Along the blue-line was written: *Merry Christmas Fenwick.*

A knock sounded at the door. Trillium opened it and in walked the Eatie, a pair of skates swinging from one hand, a hockey stick in the other. "I found these in my sock!" he said.

Fenwick threw his clothes on.

"Wait!" cried Trillium as the two were about to leave. "You forgot something."

She tossed her brother a small, heavy package wrapped in red paper and tied with a green ribbon. "Merry Christmas!"

Fenwick opened his gift, then gave his sister a big hug.

"Ahhhh!" said the Eatie, examining the present. "Licorice!"

"No," said Fenwick. "It's a puck."

"A what?"

"Come, I'll show you."

The Wounded Christmas Choirboy

DAVID WATMOUGH

The week that my little Cousin Terence joined our parish church choir was the time that Uncle Bill's dog, Skip, got caught in the grasscutter up to Tretawn Farm and had to have his leg amputated. It was also the week that Uncle Jan, Mother's older brother, retired from the blacksmith's forge he had worked for all those years and his son, Wilfrid, came back from St. German's and took the smithy over.

But what makes me remember that last week in June, 1943 in Cornwall so precisely wasn't really to do with the blacksmith's shop in St. Tudy to which I rode our farm horses for shoeing all year round; nor was it the image of that marvelous rabbiter, Skip, now reduced to one back leg when digging out a rabbit or rat in the hedge; but the unpleasant feel of my nose out of joint at Sunday Mass or Evensong when the old hags of our parish nudged each other and muttered over the new presence of Terence — and ignored me.

In choirboy terms Master Terence Menhenniot was indubitably a pin-up job. I had been what in our village of St. Keverne, the elders grudgingly conceded as "a 'andsome little bugger" as I had first set out down the Norman aisle in cotta and cassock at the age of ten. But Terence's looks were of a wholly different order.

Setting aside such ancillary factors as my being now thirteen, at the end of my chorister's tether, as it were, and with a couple of pimples to declare with my breaking voice that my ethereal days as a soprano were rapidly on the wane, eight-year-old Terence with his golden curls, had instantly turned our bevy of worshippers who were invariably inspired by malice towards mankind in general, and hatred of our High Church Vicar in particular, into besotted fans.

I suppose the situation was inevitable. For the past three years our twenty-member choir had found it progressively difficult to sustain its dozen boys, and what new faces Father Trewin had managed to dragoon into service had proved no competition for me. With their ruddy faces, straight hair, oafish manners, and squawking voices it was perfectly clear that our parish priest lay more emphasis on the presence of an adequate number of small boys in starched surplices and black cassocks than on their vocal support of the six farmers, the sexton, and the schoolmaster who provided the tenor and bass contributions to our assembly.

But in the Norman church tower, that strange place with the furry ends of the bell-ropes looped like caterpillars over our heads, and the broad slate flagstones of the floor littered with owl and bat droppings, I glumly watched Terence Menhenniot prepare for his debut in the procession to the choir stalls at the far end of the church, with all the self-conscious diligence of a Duse or Bernhardt. And in his poise and confidence as he arranged his cotta over the cassock, and fitted the ruff at his neck — all articles of ecclesiastical apparel which I knew he had never worn before in his life — I recognized both a consummate competitor for the eye of the congregation and a winner to boot.

And so it was. Mrs. Trebilcock, whose whisper was as loud as her reputation for venom was extensive, spoke across the aisle to Mrs. Harry Hoskyns — right after the first two pairs of little boys had passed her pew. "My, that Terence is a proper treat you! 'Tis lovely to have a chile as fetchin' as that one — specially after they other buggers."

I had no doubt, of course, as to the identity of "they other buggers." Only the previous Sunday I had overheard her in the church porch, telling Mr. Nankivell who farmed the Glebe, how stuck up all we Bryants were, and how boys like Rob Pengelly, Tom Purdue, Will Carthew, and me, with our reputations, shouldn't be allowed in the choir at all. "Sex fiends, they be, Mr. Nankivell. A disgrace to St. Keverne if ever there was!" And her thin mouth had slammed shut with the same moist slap mother made when putting up pounds of fresh butter on the cold slate shelves of the dairy.

I knew the old cow was referring to an unpleasant incident involving twelve-year-old Molly, Police constable Apse's daughter, who in a fit of remorse had admitted to mutual anatomical exploration with us four boys on top of Mr. Prouse's freshly made haystack. The woman's vicious attach had concluded by her remarking to Mr. Nankivell that we should be all sent packing from St. Keverne parish church — "cos they'm really nothin' but a pack of Methodies." The latter being an allusion to the fact that my Aunt Marjorie, after having told Father Trewin that she could see no reason why her five kids couldn't attend both the church and chapel Sunday School outings, had broken with the custom of most of the families in our hamlet of Churchtown and started joining the folks from up Trelill way, who heard uneducated lay preachers rant in the chapel every Sunday morning, instead of Holy Mass.

Unfortunately, Terence Menhenniot's fanclub didn't end with vile Mrs. Trebilcock and her sycophantic cronies — nor was it stimulated only by such ulterior motives as the Bryant hatred which animated her. Father Trewin, who definitely wasn't one of your child-molestors (like the Parson over Rough Tor way, who was always fiddling with his boy scouts), could be seen from his special stall across from us in choir positively *simpering* over the beauteous newcomer.

And when it transpired, at the very first practice, that my little cousin couldn't even sing on pitch, let alone carry a tune in his head, Father Trewin simply told him not to worry and that it would all come right later, if he persisted.

Then there were those men in the choir who patently favored him over the likes of Rob, Tom, Will, and me, and never watched him with the suspicion and mistrust which they seemed to think wholly in order for the likes of us who were somewhat older and certainly finer vocalists.

The situation didn't improve as Sundays and Greater Feasts passed with the Church's Calendar and those rare but fiscally profitable occasions such as important weddings or the funerals of local notables, which all warranted the choral forces of the Parish Church of St. Keverne and the Blessed Virgin Mary — to give it its full, if rarely used, title.

Each time would see young Terence faithfully present, his curly locks as gorgeous as ever, his peaches and cream complexion unblemished, and those wide grey eyes wed to that kissable cupid's bow ever raised in dutiful supplication towards the lowered cheek of authority: innocence ever at the ready to repay experience.

In the words of the scriptures which we read and sang "*and the flesh of the child waxed warm*" and like King David (of whom we knew much and with whom *I* liked to identify) young Terence "*was ruddy and beautiful.*" Moreover, Terence did develop his singing abilities as Father Trewin had prophesied, and by the end of his first year in the choir his slightly husky, alto voice could soar beyond that of any of us, and the sweetness and purity of it was so breathtakingly distinctive that (I invariably noted with a scowl) the congregation would readily start to nudge one another and that Trebilcock creature would immediately start her loud talking again.

I began to detest those days when I knew we would be singing such old favorites of mine — because I'd always been given the solos — as *I Know That My Redeemer Liveth* and *Lead Me Lord* for my voice was but a croak and it was now 'golden boy' who warbled to heaven — with or without the uncertain support of aged Miss Cleve at the organ.

Perhaps sensing that Terence was less than popular with his fellow-choristers, the boy's mother, a thin woman named Muriel, began to attend each service at which her only child now sang. She sat erect in the front pew, from where she could see him most clearly and dreamily eye the love of her life. For Muriel Menhenniot, as my mother had told me once when I was complaining about Terence's smug demeanor, had not borne her son until she was forty-two and she and her railwayman husband had despaired of ever becoming parents. That was the reason, my mother asserted, why Terence was so initially spoiled at home — although that excuse was later compounded by his mother's conviction that her golden-haired son was so delicate that he had to be shielded from the more basic crudities of village life, such as fraternizing with his coevals and even sharing the various chores which were the lot of our Cornish childhood, regardless of gender, parental wealth, or individual temperament.

So Terence was escorted twice each Sunday to church, just as he was to choir practice on Wednesday evenings. He didn't go to our village school (run by Mr. Oliver Bray who sang baritone) but to a private one where the children wore cherry-red uniforms and looked silly. And even that was not in

Wadebridge, our local town, but north of us in Camelford where he took the National bus each day.

Then again, he *never* helped out at hay-making, corn harvest, or threshing when every youngster in the parish was pressed into service; nor was he ever to be seen collecting kindling for the copper and Monday's clothes-wash, up to Tregilderns cottage behind the fig bush, where the Menhenniots lived. Instead, if you please, he was given special voice lessons with Mrs. Wesley Jago, L.R.C.M., all the way up the coast road to St. Minver, which he attended in a big Austin car hired from Hawkey's of Port Isaac. The extravagance of that was so overwhelming that at least our family openly described it as sinful — even though we weren't Methodists, and thus obsessed with money matters.

I have referred to my cousin's smugness — and indeed, he did seem so complacent, so cheerfully expectant of the world's approbation, that there were times when I would gladly have given away my prize ferret, Sam, just to see Master Terence fall arse over tip in the mound of manure I steadily fed each Saturday morning after mucking out the stables. But I have to admit that, accompanying his conviction that the world loved him, even as it treasured his looks and his voice, was an odd kind of innocence. Then if old bitches like Mrs. Trebilcock, usually acidulous men like Oliver Bray, the baritone who sat behind me in the choir, and, of course, his own adoring parents, all turned into simpering idiots when discussing him or in his company, it was surely no surprise that the kid took an awful lot for granted.

But there my charity runs dry. Age did not improve him. One year after his entry into the choir he scarcely bothered to give us, his choral companions let alone his relatives, the time of day. By his tenth birthday he was not only dictating to a usually dictatorial Father Trewin what he wanted to sing as solos at each service, but had totally ignored our traditional seating in choir, which was based on seniority, and taken over the stall right opposite the vicar — without asking permission of any of us.

Terence's haughtiness was not confined to his activities in our church. That same summer he refused, via his mother, the regular invitation to my August birthday party, which I shared with my cousin Loveday, whose nativity was but two days from mine, and which most of our young relatives attended in the mowey where tressle tables were always erected for the outdoor feast.

In summary, I hardly feel that I am exaggerating when I say that by the time I had left the boys' section of the choir altogether and had become a mere passenger with the men while waiting to discover whether I was going to end up a baritone or a tenor, Terence Menhenniot, pretty-faced star chorister, was talking (or singing, rather) only to God!

I remember what was virtually my last exchange with The Brat (as my brother Jan and I had succinctly dubbed him). It was a Wednesday night in December: the special choir rehearsal, in fact, for the December 8th Feast of Our Lady — the observance of whose Immaculate Conception had been intro-duced into our parish by its current incumbent, Father Trewin. I had overheard a recent conversation among some of our parish malcontents who objected to this rather exotic celebration. In church, just by the ancient granite font, and almost under the Great Seal of King Charles II given to those of St. Keverne for rallying to the restoration of the monarchy, I myself echoed their sentiments. "That there Immaculate Conception we'm having is really for Papists, you. 'Tidn'n exactly Church of England stuff, is it?"

But it was immediately obvious that The Brat had been well primed by the Vicar. "The Celtic Church is bravun older than Canterbury. We don't have to listen to they for what we can do and what us can't. After all, Davey, half of our saints they never heard on — including St. Keverne our patron!"

"I 'spose you got some special ole job to sing," put in Harry Purdue, my old friend Tom's younger brother. "That's why you'm a backin' of 'ee. Any ole sow-pig can see that! We b'aint born yesterday Terence Menhenniot. I bide you come only for the anthems and they descants."

"Our father says you b'aint here so much for the candlelight as the *limelight*," contributed a small boy who looked like a Cardew but I wasn't quite sure — now that there were so many of them with the ginger hair and freckles, about the place.

"I don't have to listen to none of 'ee," my cousin retorted hotly. "I'm sitting a choral scholarship if you did but know it. Then I shall be singing down to Truro Cathedral and in the choir school there. Shan't be sorry to shake the dust of his silly ole plaice off me feet, neither!"

And with that, plus a complementary toss of those curls which had turned a darker gold since he had first joined the choir, he sailed off in the direction of the church tower where all our music was untidily stacked and where the mice blithely chewed paper and left between our pages their pellets of digested pleasure.

The Feast of The Immaculate Conception of the Blessed Virgin Mary was duly celebrated according to the dictates of our parish priest, and went off without a hitch. How I loathed that fine-chiseled little face as I watched it stare up at the oak barrel-roofing of our church, as the sweet stream of sound spewed forth.

Afterwards, outside in the porch, where the Elizabethan stocks, in their wormholed antiquity, ranged the granite wall and from whose rafters rows of sleepy pipistrelle bats hung, amid a few terse and softspoken disapprovals of the service, I actually heard Muriel Menhenniot sobbing her pleasure at the transporting joy her son's voice had just afforded her. And that Terence nearly having to be immaculately conceived himself!

I wanted to vomit instead.

But fortunately I didn't and my iron self-control was very soon rewarded. We had no sooner gotten over the Immaculate Conception when we had to turn our attention to the Christmas festivities. Now that particular year what we call in our family our 'English cousins' were coming down from London to escape the Labor Government and the postwar shortages. It was what they called 'Austerity' up there and my mother felt that her sister and family would benefit from a bit or Cornish cooking and all the fresh farm and dairy produce that were available to us, as well as a few of the early vegetables from Penzance and The Scillies that would have cost the earth up to London.

Apart from the minor upheaval of stretching the resources of Polengarrow farm to contain ten people instead of the normal five, it also meant that my first cousin, Arthur, whom I had last seen as a baby, would be arriving. Well, he not only arrived, looking incredibly like a younger version of Terence to whom he was distantly related, but immediately asked whether he would be able to sing in our choir on Christmas morning, as he would have done in Wimbledon church had he stayed at home.

Although I wasn't minded to like small boys, let alone aid their requests, in this case I acted without hesitation. "I do know for a fact that we'm shorthanded down there," I told Arthur, "so I'll slip right down to the Vicarage on me bike and ask Father Trewin if he'll have on 'ee."

Just as I expected, there was no prevarication from that quarter. In fact not only the Vicar, but everyone else with whom I spoke during those days leading up to the holidays, seem strangely elated at the prospect of young Arthur's presence in the chancel of St. Keverne Church. Unusual in that our villagers were disinclined to welcome strangers — even the kin of those who had lived among them for centuries, as had we Bryants.

At Christmastide in St. Keverne's Church that year we went full out. The rood screen was garlanded not only with the traditional evergreens, the holly and the ivy, but we even managed to scour the protected hedgerows and dells of the immediate countryside to yield a few early primroses and we also had some hardy roses from Uncle Joe Yelland's cottage with its secluded southern aspect, plus some usual winter jasmine from our farmhouse garden. The latter made a rich yellow frieze about the font and behind the altar of the Lady Chapel.

In 1947, I recall, we still had only candles and oil lamps for illumination as my Great Uncle Herbert didn't provide electricity (in memory of his wife) until the following year. But what with the sumptuous musical setting for Midnight Mass and the decorative efforts extending over three days by the women of the parish, even little Arthur, with all his London sophistication, was entranced with what he saw when the two of us entered the church the afternoon of Christmas Eve. We were there because our young visitor had asked if he might have a prior look at the music as he had been unable to attend earlier choir practices — a professional attention to detail, I duly noted, that far exceeded anything that Terence had ever demonstrated.

All my hopeful anticipations over Arthur were realized from the very moment the solemn procession of Christmas, including the blessing of the crib, wound us up and down the shadowy aisles to the words and tune of the hymn, *Adeste Fideles*. Not only did his animated face, bathed in the soft glow of oil lamps, yield an innocence and piety which made the overly familiar Terence look positively corrupt, but Wimbledon's soprano quite blotted out in range and sweetness the efforts of Master Menhenniot. And if it was thus in the opening hymn, it was ever more so as the Liturgy unfolded. By the time we reached the Plainsong Setting of that lovely phrase from the Gradual, *"the dew of thy birth is of the womb of the morning,"* Terence had succumbed to the sulks and was silent while the rest of the boys gladly followed suit to allow the full force of Arthur's mastery of Gregorian chant, and ethereality of tone, to fill first the candle-bright choir stalls and sanctuary and then the great length of the nave itself. I looked quickly in the direction of Father Trewin, hoping that the priest was at least acknowledging that a greater than Terence had come among us and was gratified to observe the old man's eyes opening and closing in ecstasy. Leering by now in triumph, I turned to feast on the expressions of my fellow-choirmen: white heads and bald ones nodded in grave appreciation of the newcomer in our midst.

Nor was Arthur's devastating effect confined to those of us on the altar side of the rood screen. Out in the packed congregation, Cornish souls melted in the flow of such vocal beauty as my cousin from across the Tamar so felicitously bestowed. In the soft candlelight of the sanctuary Arthur Ingram's features held the delicacy of a Michelangelo sculpture as he soared in descant after descant and solo'd the Plainsong when the older music of the Church usurped the more recent hymns.

Mrs. Trebilcock was seen to take a handkerchief from her large handbag and sob noisly into it and towards the end of the Eucharist — when the Wimbledon nightingale transported us finally on that wondrous and memorable night with the verses of *Once in Royal David's City* soaked in his own special purity — history in St. Keverne parish was made when, from isolated spots in the congregation, came the sound of enthusiastic clapping.

Wholly unnerved by the applause, a horrified Vicar gulped his blessing from the altar, and Miss Cleve, in panic (transmitted no doubt by her parish priest), laid too many digits upon the console, causing the organ to sound briefly like a ship's klaxon in a dense fog. The rest, I confess, was anti-climax.

Young Terence, bud-mouth clamped tight, fairly bolted his exit in the final procession down the church to the belltower where we were routinely prayed over and dismissed. But that early Christmas morn Terence didn't linger longer than to yank off his cotta and tear at the multiple buttons of his cassock — as if the garment, too, were an offence not to be borne. Even as Father Trewin muttered a final Hail Mary, our erstwhile star of the choir stalls was pushing open the heavy oak door, tear-glistening eyes in a head held defiantly high.

I did not know then, of course, but he was never to sing in our choir again. In fact that was but the least of it for our toppled alto. For the next several days I put him quite out of mind as young Arthur and his relatives were our preoccupation. But after the Ingrams had left and the wintry rhythms of January had taken over, it gradually became apparent that not only was Terry now missing from choir-practices and the Sunday services, but he was no longer to be seen anywhere in the village. I mentioned this to Mother who in turn informed me that when Father Trewin visited the Menhenniots to enquire after Terence, he was refused entry at Tregilderns cottage by the boy himself who began to scream and shout until the old priest turned sadly away.

I am sure that I would have thought a good deal less about Cousin Terence, now that he was no longer visible, had it not been for a distressing occurrence that March when his father met with a terrible accident at the entrance to the railway tunnel, just south of Port Isaac Road station. Severely mangled as a result of falling between the cars of a freight train, he was taken by ambulance to Tehiddy hospital where he survived for only three days. At the funeral down to St. Keverne, it was noted with shock and incredulity that a sobbing widow was unaccompanied by a mourning son. Muriel Menhenniot, almost hysterical in grief, relied on the succouring ministrations of old Mrs. Trethewey, her next door neighbor, and it was she who led the distraught woman out of the church before the Requiem was concluded.

After that there were many who presented themselves at the cottage behind the fig bush and fuchsia hedge to offer the two remaining Menhenniots their services. But none crossed the threshold. Either the black-clad Muriel or a progressively dissheveled Terence refused the world entry and shouted and screamed until obeyed. Eventually they were left alone. I recall talk of the district nurse visiting and even mention of a psychiatrist. But that is all rather vague by now. Certainly I never set eyes on Terence again during the remainder of his childhood and youth.

Whether the result of his savage fall from a stellar role in the choir, or the tragedy of his father's premature death, one can only speculate, but the fact remains that the Christmas of 1947 was virtually the last that Terence Menhenniot was seen beyond the confines of Tregilderns and its leafy garden.

It was in 1967 that Mother wrote to me in Vancouver, where I had settled some years earlier, and informed me that Muriel had recently passed on — Mother's letters were little more than St. Keverne obituary lists by this time — and that the stout, balding man who had stood alone as Chief Mourner at her burial service was none other than Terence. Immediately after the commital in the upper graveyard (where she lay flanked by her husband, Fred, and my second cousin Lewis) he left without exchanging a word with anyone save Ned Carhart, the stone mason, about a tombstone — presumably back to Tregilderns and its quiet behind that enormous fig bush.

One other snippet Mother added to her airletter. Terence was now a practiced ham radio operator and, according to village gossip, often stayed up all night talking via his microphone to people all over the world.

A Migrant Christmas

JANE RULE

Harry wasn't the one in the family who had a principle against doing what everyone else did. It was his wife, Anna, who liked to be out of sync with everyone else, whether for buying a house or starting a family; so Harry never seemed to have either the problems or the pleasures his friends did, both his children and his mortgage years younger. Mike's son was dealing dope before Joey had tried a cigarette behind the garage, and Al's daughter was in danger of pregnancy before Sally learned to read.

"Well, it gets worse before it gets better," Al philosophized. "The best thing about kids is that they grow up and leave home."

"Joyce and I have an even better solution. We're growing up and leaving home first. We're going to Mexico for January," Mike announced.

It wasn't just that Joey and Sally were too young to leave alone. Harry frankly couldn't imagine a holiday without them. Even the year Anna had talked them into going to Europe, Joey was less than a year old and went everywhere on Harry's back. Harry still couldn't eat an ice cream cone without expecting a second tongue to help. He and Anna were far too old to take a holiday on their own and still be able to stop at every advertised snake pit and haunted house along the way. Harry would feel like a fool going into one of those child-sized motel swimming pools by himself, and he didn't suppose you ever took just your wife out for a hamburger even if, like Anna, she happened to love them.

No, he didn't envy Mike and Joyce their freedom from the children for a month, but he did envy them their winter holiday. Wouldn't it be really good for Anna and the kids to have at leat a couple of weeks out of the rain sometimes tipping to snow, in the winter sun? They wouldn't have to drive all the way to Mexico. Anna was good with languages, so good it had been sometimes hard for Harry not to feel unmanned by her confident handling of their lives all the time they were on the continent. Her stomach was as admirable as her tongue. She hadn't taken one Lomatil in the months they were in Europe. There were weeks when Harry ate nothing else. Montezuma's revenge, and therefore Mexico, had no part in Harry's daydream.

"People in wheelchairs take winter holidays," Anna said over after-dinner coffee at the kitchen table while the children made a quarrelsome game of the dishes.

"Mike and Joyce don't even have a golf cart," Harry protested.

"Oh, it's because Mike and Joyce . . ."

"It is not. It is nothing of the kind. I want to do just what they're not doing. I want to take the kids along, go when we can all enjoy it together."

"What about school?" Joey asked.

"Might keep you out of trouble for a while after you got back," Anna suggested.

Their problem with Joey was that he was too good in school, his patience more often tested than either his mind or imagination.

"Then you like the idea?" Harry asked, encouraged.

"Could I take Petey?" Sally asked.

"I don't think birds are allowed to cross the border," Harry said.

It was one of those remarks that sent all three others into rounds of laughter which mildly puzzled Harry.

"It's — like — birds, Dad," Joey then said kindly. "Going south. Petey could migrate in his cage."

Mike had already taken January, and the office was too short-staffed for Harry to have a holiday at the same time.

"Go for Christmas," his boss said.

"All right," Anna agreed.

"We aren't going to miss Christmas, Sally," Harry explained. "Everywhere is Christmas."

"Will it snow?"

"No. We'll probably go swimming on Christmas day, just the way they do in Australia."

"Can we cut our own tree?"

"It will be a cactus. Now, look, you guys, the point is something different, all right?"

"Christmas isn't exactly boring the way it is," Joey said.

"It's time they traveled," Harry said later when the children had gone to bed. "They're in a rut already."

"Well, kids are conservative about greed, that's all," Anna said. "They don't want to get out of the range of Santa Claus. You can understand that."

"Since it's Christmas, do you think, just this once, we might try for reservations?"

"No," Anna said. What she had refused to do all through

crowded Europe, she was not about to agree to in the sparsely populated southern desert.

"If there's no room at the inn?"

"We stay in the stable. Anyway, who but a family of nuts goes away for Christmas?"

"Jews. Every Jew I know is trying to get his kids away from Christmas."

"Happy Hanukkah," Anna said and yawned.

The only elaborate preparations Harry tried to make were those for Sally's canary, but, though he called every office from embassy to customs, he could get neither Canada nor the United States to object to taking Petey with them. The bird had as much right to go south as they did.

"You don't even want a certificate from the vet?" Harry asked, incredulous.

"Not even proof of citizenship."

Harry finally resorted to reasoning with Sally. "What if the weather confuses him? What if he begins to molt?"

But Sally, at five, could be as implacable as her mother.

"The bird," Anna reminded Harry, "was your idea in the first place."

Harry had one of those clairvoyant moments about the trip, his idea in the first place, during which impossible-to-imagine responsibilities and problems would fall to him to bear and solve. How he wished it had been Anna's suggestion against which he could raise all that might be impractical and ominous.

Joey, once he'd brought home his first book about the desert, was Harry's enthusiastic ally.

"There are rattlesnakes and flash floods," Joey promised them all. "And much better earthquakes than we ever have."

He didn't scare Anna, who was a fatalist, but he terrified Sally with stories of carnivorous birds and aggressive cacti.

"You know, you can't treat a cactus like a tree, Dad," Joey explained. "They're more like porcupines." And to Sally he said, "You don't even have to touch some of them to make them shoot their quills at you."

"We're going to be picking grapefruit and oranges off the trees," Harry said. "We're going to be lying in the sun. We're going to be swimming and playing golf and tennis."

"I don't know how, most of those," Sally said.

"I'll teach you."

In the spirit of their escape from winter, Harry tried to curse their first snow, which fell only several days before they were to leave, but with the new snow tires he'd bought for mountain driving, he had no trouble getting home, and the kids were out on the hill with garbage can lids having a lovely time.

"This is going to be cake-and-eat-it year," Harry said confidently.

"It's hard to look out the window and then pack shorts and bathing suits," Anna said.

She did not go on to compare the experience with daffodils on the Christmas dinner table, of which she didn't approve.

"I've told them we're not hauling all our presents down there and back. We'll have a second Christmas when we get home, all right?"

"I guess so," Harry said.

It was not practical, of course, with limited room in the car, with customs, but he was not sure, come the day itself, how he'd be Santa Claus without presents.

"Well, one each," Anna said, modestly relenting.

Petey was the only one to get his present early, a traveling cage a foot square with a light-tight cover.

"It's not just to shut him up at night," Anna explained. "It's to keep him from getting car sick."

"Do birds get car sick?" Harry asked, incredulous.

"They don't get seasick," Joey said, "or gulls wouldn't ride on the ferry boats."

"Is Petey going to throw up?" Sally asked.

"How about leaving him home?"

"Just because I get car sick, you don't leave me home," Sally answered indignantly.

It snowed again the morning they were to leave, but nobody minded, and Harry presented them all with new plaid laprobes for the occasion.

"I wanted to get beach towels," he confessed, "but there weren't any around this time of year."

The children were warmly settled in the back seat, cool can between them in which Anna had packed all they needed for breakfasts and lunches along the way, Petey in his covered cage on top of that. Anna was in front with her knitting.

"We're off," Harry said, as the wheels spun for a second before the new tires grabbed and sent them in a jolt out of the driveway.

Harry had planned three days for the trip. At the end of the first, he wondered if they'd ever get there at all. It had taken them twelve hours to get to Portland. He sometimes hadn't been able to see more than fifteen feet in front of him, and patches of ice made braking no option, as the huge double trailer trucks jack-knifed across the road testified.

"Wow, look at that!" Joey would exclaim, peering through the snow veil. "Is it going to blow up, do you think, Dad?"

Sally thought it wasn't fair not to let Petey see something of the trip, but, when she uncovered him and found him huddled in the corner of the tiny cage, his feathers fluffed out like a winter overcoat, she didn't have to be told to cover him again.

"Is he going to die?" she asked every fifteen or twenty minutes.

They hadn't dared to stop for lunch, not only because they might have frozen to death, but because there was no sure way off the road. The others ate, but Harry managed no more than half a sandwich and a couple of swigs of Anna's vegetable soup which sat, a sour fist of fear, in his stomach for the rest of the day. He couldn't even eat the hamburgers he finally managed to buy them after they were safely installed in a Portland motel.

If the heat had worked, if the ice machine hadn't kept him awake most of the night, Harry might have been tempted to suggest they hole in there until the storm — or winter — was over.

"We ought to be out of this in another day," Anna said reassuringly.

"Mike and Joyce *fly* to Mexico," Harry said grimly.

"We're doing what they're not doing," Anna reminded him.

Half way through Oregon, the snow turned to rain, but at Grant's Pass it was snowing again, and Harry was told by the motel manager that both roads into California were closed.

"For how long?"

There was no way of telling. This motel room was, at least, warm, but it wasn't until the next afternoon during the seventh game of monopoly that the sun finally came out and Petey began to sing. Though they had paid for a second night, Harry decided right after dinner, when he heard the roads were open, to leave at once. It would be the hardest part of the trip for Sally, the road twisting down out of the mountains, and this way she might sleep through it. After she threw up her dinner at a snow-narrowed turn out, she did, and Harry resisted taking up her question about the distressed bird. As they crossed the California border, they slowed to go through the inspection station where they had to give up the mandarin oranges they'd forgotten to declare at the international border. It seemed to Harry another symbolic deprivation of their Canadian Christmas.

"I thought there were orange and grapefruit trees in California," Joey said, peering out at the dark evergreen forests so like what they had left behind.

"There will be, son," Harry said determinedly.

At dawn, the first miracle of the trip occurred. There on

either side of the road were the promised orange and grapefruit groves, bright with fruit lovelier than ornaments on a Christmas tree, acres and acres of them.

"Look," Joey said, "there's fruit on the ground. Could we . . . ?"

"Waste not, want not," Anna said to Harry who was always dubious about anything that might not be law abiding.

So he stopped, and they all got out and picked up oranges which were more fragrant and tasted sweeter than any Harry remembered since his childhood. So peacefully euphoric was he to have brought his family safely out of the winter storms of the north to this amazing morning that he said aloud what he had nearly decided not to mention.

"Old Carl lives in Bakersfield."

Anna did not respond.

"Who's old Carl?" Sally asked.

"A friend of mine," Harry said, preparing to regret his remark.

Carl was the sort of friend you had until you got seriously enough involved with a woman to introduce them and within moments of seeing Carl in a woman's eyes, even the most tolerant sort of woman, you wondered what you had ever seen in him at all, for he was fat, loud, and stupid. Yet, because Harry hadn't seen Carl in ten years, his memory went back to those times before Anna when Carl had been one of Harry's gang of to-hell with-it college buddies, willing to go to any game, movie, night club, on any drunk, willing to take his car and spend his money.

"He's married now. He's got kids," Harry said. "Might just give him a call, stop for a drink on our way through, since it's Christmas time."

Anna still didn't comment. Joey was watching her; then he turned to his father and shrugged. "It's okay with me."

Carl was, indeed, delighted to hear Harry's voice on the phone, gave him instructions in confused detail about how to get to the house, told him to come for a drink, come for dinner, spend the night, whatever.

"We are not going to impose on that man's poor wife," Anna began.

"Of course not," Harry agreed. "We'll just drop in and say hello."

"Could we have a cookie?" Sally asked.

"If you're offered one," Anna said.

"They'll probably be coconut," Joey suggested brightly; he loved coconut, and Sally wouldn't touch it.

It was one of the dozen times a day the strategically placed cool can kept marginal peace with Petey functioning as a sort of one-bird UN force.

When they arrived at the door, Carl opened it and said, much less enthusiastically than on the phone, "Come in and all, but my wife says to tell you the boy has mumps, so if your kids . . ."

"I've had the mumps," Joey said.

"Sally, darling," Anna said. "You'll have to wait in the car. We'll only be a few minutes."

Sally's face filled up with tears like a glass at a tap.

"You don't want to be sick for Christmas."

"There isn't going to be any Christmas," she wailed.

"Look, maybe we better make it another time," Harry began.

"At least, come in and see the tree," Carl said. "Otherwise, I'm stuck here with my mother-in-law all afternoon."

"I heard that, Carl!" shouted a deep, sexless voice from inside the room. "It's a question of who's stuck with who."

At the sound of that voice, the tears began to drain out of Sally's face.

'I *think* I've had mumps," Joey said.

"Look," Harry said, "both of you go back to the car, all right? We won't be long."

He and Anna were back in twenty minutes.

"What did the tree look like?" Sally demanded.

"Just like a tree," Harry said, "cluttering up the living room."

"Were there presents?"

"Were there cookies?"

"Mostly there were sick kids and crabby relatives."

"Was the lady inside a witch?"

"More or less," Harry said. "Now, aren't you glad we're not having a Christmas like that?"

"We don't have crabby relatives," Sally said.

"How fat do you suppose that guy is?" Joey said.

"Even fatter than I remembered," Harry said.

Though he was promising himself not to remember anything on his own before Anna again ever, he was also feeling modestly smug about his own decent shape, his good-looking and agreeable wife, his healthy children. "Poor old Carl. Some people are born to make other people feel good."

"Good?" Anna asked.

"Well, better," Harry clarified.

On the outskirts of town, he found a motel with a kidney-shaped pool, and he slept in the California sun while Anna and the children played in the water.

The next day in Palm Springs, they all did some secretive Christmas shopping.

"Let's get the kids a *piñata*," Anna suggested. "We're nearly at the Mexican border."

Once they had taken advantage of the stores, Harry was restless to be on their way.

"You mean, this isn't where we're going?" Anna asked.

"You don't want to stay here, do you?" Harry asked, surprised.

"Where else in there?"

"The state park. Borrego Springs. It has everything Palm Springs has except Palm Springs."

Not until they were leaving town and Anna began to sing carols did Harry realize she'd been resigning herself to a week in that rich resort town where private guard services protected the mostly deserted houses of celebrities, where the chief conversation among the locals seemed to be skin cancer, and the tourists complained about the prices of flowered trousers. Harry had not spoken of Borrego Springs before because he wanted to seem spontaneous while being prepared. They would be in the real desert in a little community with, nevertheless, plenty of tourist accommodations, well before dark on Christmas Eve.

As they all sang together *We Three Kings*, Harry heard Sally's high, sweet version of "of Oreo Tar." His cookie-obsessed daughter did not get in the way of his fantasy that they could be that new breed of agnostic wise men still following a star across the badlands in the delicate winter light to a simple place, to a yearly miracle.

"Wow!" Joey said. "Did you see that sign? 'This Road Is Subject to Flash Floods'!"

Each time they dipped into a dry wash, Joey looked in vain for the rushing water. Then he saw a road runner with a snake's tail hanging out of its beak.

"Those big ones look like they're on fire," Sally said as they passed twelve-foot-high ocotillos, their bare, viciously thorned limbs tipped by fragile red bloom.

Anna's hand rested on Harry's thigh. "I like the ones with halos," she said, nodding to crowns of bright thorns.

Then there before them, nearly at the foot of western mountains, as bare of vegetation as a dinosaur's hide, was the oasis of Borrego Springs, green with golf courses, punctuated by date palms.

The two motels near the stores were full. The next three didn't take pets or children.

"No children?" Harry asked each time. "You've got to be

kidding. And the bird's in a cage."

He drove them back into the center and found a real estate office.

"I'm willing to rent a house if I have to," Harry explained, trying to sound reasonable.

"To have children in it, you'd have to buy one," the sales man explained. "Even then you couldn't buy one at any of the clubs."

"What are you, paranoid about school taxes or something? Didn't Proposition Thirteen take care of that?"

"This is a retirement community and an adult resort."

"You could camp in the park," a gas station attendant suggested. "There's no objection to kids in the park."

"It gets down to forty degrees," Harry protested. "We've got nothing with us but lap robes."

"I'd say your best bet is to go back to Palm Springs or over to San Diego."

"We want to stay here."

Sally was staring out the window watching a white-haired woman pedal a giant tricycle up the street.

"This is a funny place," she said. "She isn't really children, is she?"

"There aren't any children," Joey explained.

"Did they die?"

"They aren't allowed."

Harry got a list of every place in the valley that offered accommodation. He stood putting dimes into the pay phone as if it were a slot machine.

"Surely, on Christmas Eve you'd make an exception," he'd try. Then exasperated, he'd begin to shout, "Children have rights, too, you know!"

"Harry," Anna finally said, "I think we better get out of here."

"I'm starving," Joey said. "Are kids allowed to eat here?"

"There's that little Mexican restaurant," Anna said. "How about some tacos, and then we'll drive over to the ocean."

The place was jammed. They had to stand to wait their turn and were finally seated at a table for ten, otherwise occupied by aging couples.

"What are people doing, eating out on Christmas Eve?" Harry whispered angrily to Anna. "They ought to be at home with their grandchildren."

But Anna was exchanging friendly greetings with the old man next to her.

"Nice to see a couple of kids," he was saying. "I said to my wife — this is Rachel, my wife — funny place with no kids around, quiet as the grave."

"Oh, Sam, don't exaggerate. There are children right next door to us. We're renting. We just come down from Oregon for a month," she confided to Anna, "and renters can't have children, but owners are allowed to have grandchildren visit."

"It's unnatural!" Harry said.

When Sam and Rachel heard the dilemma that faced these Canadian visitors, they were as irate as Harry and agreed that it was not only unnatural but un-American, and they would do something about it.

"Listen," Sam said. "We've got plenty of space, twin beds in the spare room, a second bathroom, big fold-out bed in the living room."

"But children aren't allowed," Harry reminded him.

"We'll just smuggle them in," Rachel decided. "When we finish here," she continued in a lowered voice, "we'll put the children in our car under a blanket. Then a little while later, you come along . . ."

"What about Petey?" Sally asked.

"We have a canary," Harry said glumly.

"If we can smuggle a couple of kids, who's worried about a canary?"

"But you could get evicted," Harry reminded them.

"So that's the end of the world?" Sam asked.

"You're wonderful," Anna said, "Thank you."

Once the plan was approved, all six of them took their parts with elaborate seriousness. Harry insisted on paying the whole bill while Rachel and Sam took the children and hid them under their own lap robes on the back seat of their large and impressive American car.

"God, I hope they're not kidnappers," Anna said suddenly as the old couple drove off.

"You're the one who agreed!" Harry shouted, rushing to their own car.

When Anna got in beside him, she was laughing. Then she said, "I'm sorry about being so dumb about making reservations."

"I would have settled for a stable if I could have found one."

They found the car parked in the carport of number one-hundred-and-thirty-one in the mobile home park, and they found the children in the living room, eating cookies. Harry put Petey in his covered cage on top of the television set.

"They'll think it's on TV," Rachel said, "whatever noise we make. As long as we keep the curtains closed, and the kids stay off the screened porch."

Anna helped Rachel make up the guest room beds and then settled the children while Harry accepted a drink and a look around, never having been inside these giant kleenex boxes on wheels before.

"Come say goodnight," Anna called.

"Dad," Sally said, "you said Christmas was everywhere."

"And so it is," Harry said, smiling at his clean, comfortable children as safely settled as they might have been with grandparents.

"I don't see any tree. I don't see any presents."

"Well, older people, on their own, sometimes . . ."

"The thing is, Sally," Anna interrupted. "Sam and Rachel are Jewish, and Jewish people don't celebrate Christmas."

"Jewish people don't believe in Santa Claus?" Sally asked. "I don't really either, but everybody can pretend."

"Jews don't believe in Jesus," Joey said.

"Neither exactly do we," Anna said. "There are a lot of different ways to believe in kindness and hope and love. There'll be surprises in the morning. Just don't worry about it."

Out in the living room where Rachel was making up their bed, another worried conversation had obviously taken place.

"Rachel says we can make a tree out of palm fronds," Sam explained. "And . . . "

"You mustn't go to any trouble," Anna protested. "We came away partly to get away from all the elaborate fuss Christmas gets to be. We're not really believers either."

At that moment, they heard the voices of carolers outside the door, mostly wandering old voices with one true soprano, singing of a child born to Mary, and they all went out to listen.

"We're not all that much Jews either," Sam said as they went back into the house. "Anyway, there's no real way to get away from Christmas, not with kids in the house."

The courteous argument turned into the joy of finding palm fronds in the desert moonlight for the men, baking for the women. It was nearly as late as it always got at home when Sam and Rachel finally retired to their bedroom, leaving Harry and Anna to sleep in the splendor of a room-high tree of palm fronds, decorated with dozens of freshly baked and brightly frosted cookies, presents for everyone stacked underneath it, Harry's gift to Anna and hers to him re-labeled for Sam and Rachel, the piñata hanging over the breakfast table.

Harry woke at dawn, for a moment uncertain where he was until he saw the tree, and he was very glad that he had a wife who believed in miracles rather than reservations, that Christmas would be as secret and illicit as it had been in the beginning, for the sake of the children. He got up and opened the curtains just a crack. Then he took the cover off Petey and let him sing. Outside a mocking bird in the ocotillo answered that caged, illegal carol.

One More Wiseman

DAVID HELWIG

The only warning I got was a telegram from Montreal. It said "ARRIVING TOMORROW LOVE JACOB." Just that after five years.

The last time I'd seen him was in England, in a London Tube station, Tottenham Court Road I think it was. We were taking trains going in different directions, and as we separated, Jacob grinned back at me. He was wearing a heavy overcoat that made him look like a bear, and his teeth were very white in the middle of his dark beard.

"I'll see you tonight," he said.

The next day I got a telegram from Rome. It said "COME TO ITALY LOVE JACOB." Then two years of silence while I poked away at England and finally packed my life in a bag and came back to Toronto. Then three more years, happy enough, I suppose, with a job that was not too demanding and not too rewarding, a few friendships, and most recently, an arrangement of sorts with Laura, something that could have ended in marriage but hadn't.

Laura had been a widow for a year and a half now, and I had

known her for about a year. We had spent gradually more time together as the months went on. I let things happen, but never seemed to act, to be in control. Her dead husband was a presence that I could not exorcize. I had never known him, Laura never mentioned him. And I did not ask. So his presence continued to haunt us. The only honest one, I sometimes thought, was Laura's nine-year-old daughter Cathy, who disliked me because I was not her father, and she would allow no replacement. Laura and I went on, politely, foolishly, as friends. I didn't tell her that I loved her, didn't ask her to marry me. I don't know quite what I was waiting for, but I was still waiting.

Now Jacob was about to arrive in my quiet world. Over the last three years I had received two letters from him, one saying that he was separating from his wife and another two days later asking whether he'd ever written to say he was married. It was three days before Christmas when I got his telegram, and I assumed he was planning to stay with me over the holiday. The next morning I decided I would get some extra food and liquor in, to be ready to celebrate his return.

Jacob, my old friend, how to tell about him, where to start? I think I met him when we were both ten years old. It seems to me that he was a fat, grinning ten-year-old boy with a thick dark beard, standing on a street-corner, in the snow maybe, and laughing. It was always hard for me to keep the facts straight in my mind where Jacob was concerned.

His father, who had left Austria for political reasons, directed the United Church choir in which Jacob and I sang, I in a remarkably high soprano and Jacob in a rough but powerful contralto. His mother was a round smiling woman who baked buns and bread and cookies and cakes and pies and pastries and loved to see us eat them. She kept Jacob almost as round as she was herself by filling him with her food.

And Jacob, my friend for years. He had a brown sweater with a hawk on it. He had an old short wave radio. The biggest collection of Captain Marvel comic books in town. A single copy of a sunbathing magazine full of naked women. When we got to the age for real girls, he would tell me everything, and I would tell him nothing.

Holding Jacob's telegram in my hand, I looked out the window of my apartment and saw a Christmas wreath in a lighted window across the road. I remembered how we had loved Christmas. When we sang carols in church, Jacob insisted on singing the melody instead of the dull contralto harmonies that the hymn book offered him. And I, not to be outdone, would invent soaring descants. We would look across the choir loft at each other and only keep from laughing because we loved the singing, especially the wild joyful carols, *Joy to the World* or *O Come All Ye Faithful*.

As I stood there, I decided I'd better phone Laura. I was expected to spend Christmas Eve and Christmas Day with them, and I thought I should tell her (did I mean warn her?) about Jacob's coming.

I phoned, and as I knew she would, she said to bring him with me, perhaps a bit apprehensive or not really happy about it, but determined to do the right thing. I like to talk to Laura on the phone, she has a nice voice, but this time I let the conversation die quickly because I didn't want to say too much about Jacob or try to make her imagine him. I have lots of funny stories about him, but he becomes unreal in the stories, and there's some kind of disloyalty in telling them. Anyway she'd meet him soon enough. Let her judge for herself. I had a suspicion she wouldn't like him. He certainly wasn't like any of her friends. I put on a record and sat staring out the window, wondering what Jacob had been doing for the last five years, what I was going to do for the next twenty-five.

In the morning I found myself a bit puzzled about when he might arrive, and whether I should make any attempt to meet him. He might be coming by train or plane, even by car for all

I knew. There was nothing to do but tape a note on the door saying I'd be back at five-thirty and set off to work.

It was a busy morning and at noon I forgot to buy extra groceries, but I left early and arrived home just before five-thirty with my arms full of food and liquor. As I walked up to the door of my apartment, I could hear music from inside, *Gottes Zait ist die allerbaste Ziet* sung by a choir and a loud extra baritone. My arms were full, and I wasn't sure I could get my key without putting everything down so I knocked on my own door and waited.

The door opened and Jacob's familiar bearded face smiled at me. He had the same bright, scrubbed look that I remembered, and the same tattered clothes.

"Jerry," he said, "it's great, goddamit it's great."

I could see he wanted to shake my hand or throw his arm around my shoulders, but he couldn't really get at me for the bags. I went into the kitchen to put them down.

"How did you get in?" I said. "I didn't think the caretaker would ever open up for you."

"That's a funny thing," he said. "I was standing there at the door looking at your note and figuring how much trouble I'd have getting anyone to let me in or even finding out where you work when I noticed the lock was made by a company in Germany that I used to work for. That particular design has a weakness. If you know about it you can take it apart from outside. I put it back together after I got in."

"Same old Jacob," I said.

Then suddenly I didn't know what to say anymore. It was five years and I was different. I didn't know where to start.

"It's great," Jacob said again.

"Do you want a drink?" I said.

"Yeah," he said, "I want a drink."

We drank and talked a bit and then drank some more and then ate, and within a couple of hours, it had all come back so that we didn't have to think of things to talk about. He was surprised that I'd never got married. I was surprised that he had. I wanted to tell him something about Laura, but I held off for a long time. When I did mention her, he wanted me to describe her, and I tried, said she was small but not really small, had brown hair with a bit of grey coming now, and then gave up and told him to wait and see. He let it go at that, and we talked about other things, his family, my family, five years of time, and as we got drunker and more relaxed, sat in the dark listening to music and talking less. Sometime after midnight Jacob suddenly stood up and turned to me.

"This Laura," he said, "she's a widow, not young and innocent, so you must go to bed together, eh? I mean there's nothing wrong with you is there?"

"Dammit Jacob," I said, "why don't you mind your own business? Of course we go to bed together sometimes, and of course there's nothing wrong with me. Is there anything wrong with you?"

"Not a damn thing," he said. "But what I want to know is why you don't marry her?"

"I don't know why. Maybe we don't want to get married." I was shouting a little.

"Don't get touchy," he said.

"I'm not," I said. "I'm just going to bed."

I had an extra bedroom that I used for a study, and the bed there was made up so I only had to turn on the light and point to it before I wandered back to my own room and fell into bed. The last thing I remember was hearing Jacob talking to himself.

I didn't wake till almost eight o'clock. I got organized in a hurry and left Jacob a note saying I'd be home about four. There was a party at the office, but I planned to leave early.

When I got home that afternoon, it was later than I'd expected, and I only had time to wash up before we drove to Laura's for dinner. During the short drive over, Jacob asked more questions about her and I tried to answer them. He didn't seem to be listening to what I was saying.

When we got to the house, it was Cathy who answered the door, very polite and mature, giving away nothing. I wondered, as I often did when I saw her, whether she ever cried over silly things. Laura came in, wearing an apron, and apologized for not meeting us at the door. Because I'd been trying to describe her to Jacob the night before, I kept noticing things I could have mentioned: she has brown eyes and a funny mouth, she looks good in an apron through I don't know why, she's good at covering how she feels. I introduced her to Jacob and tried not to notice how they reacted to each other. I kept telling myself that it didn't matter. Two days from now Jacob would disappear and not come back for years. Still I caught myself listening to them. They didn't have much to talk about, but they seemed to want to be friends. I gave Laura the bottle of wine I had brought, and we all had a drink before she went back to the kitchen.

After we'd spent a few minutes sitting around, Jacob had the bright idea of asking Cathy to show him the house. At first she didn't want to, but before long she started to enjoy it. As we followed her about, Jacob carried the wine bottle with him and drank from it every couple of minutes. The part that Cathy enjoyed most was showing us the cellar. She had to ask her mother if she could go down, and I guess because it was an unusual thing her excitement started to show. She even relaxed enough to tell us how old the house was and that there was an old cistern under the kitchen. Jacob wanted to see that too, and the pair of them got quite involved over it. I could see that Cathy was starting to like Jacob, and I felt a bit jealous. After they were through with the cistern, Jacob wanted to see the furnace and the fuel tank.

"For God's sake, Jacob," I said, "you don't want to see the furnace."

"Of course I do," Jacob said with a big smile. "When I see a house I want to see everything. Don't you think that's right Cathy?"

"I guess so," she said, but I'm not sure she really agreed.

Jacob had a good poke around the furnace and we went back upstairs. Cathy had already eaten, and Laura got her off to bed before she served the dinner. It was a fine meal, and Jacob did it credit. He made me think of his mother's huge meals as he crouched behind his plate chewing happily, warm and content, like a stove that took in food for its fuel and gave out some rare spiritual host. Every now and then he would wink at me, and I was puzzled, but assumed that he was just expressing his delight in Laura and the food.

It was with the coffee that I started to feel cold, and by the time we had done the dishes, I was shivering and so was Laura. She went to turn up the thermostat, but when she did, nothing happened.

"Must be something wrong with the furnace," Jacob said. He seemed pleased. "I'm beautiful on furnaces," he said and headed downstairs.

"Does he know what he's doing?" Laura whispered to me.

I shrugged. There was some soft noise from the cellar, then a loud noise and the sound of Jacob running upstairs.

"Bit of a problem," he said. "I punched a hole in the fuel line somehow. I don't think there's anything to set it off, but maybe we better get out anyway. We can drive over to Jerry's place after we phone the firemen and the furnace people."

"Jacob," I said, "did you really?"

He nodded his head.

"Laura better get Cathy."

Laura looked as though she didn't know whether to be mad or scared, but she went to get Cathy. When she was gone, Jacob turned to me with a big smile.

"Beautiful eh?" he whispered.

"You didn't do that on purpose?"

He nodded.

"I figured what's nicer than to have all your friends at your place for Christmas. You and Laura and Cathy are all too well-organized."

"You're out of your goddam head."

He grinned. I could hear Laura coming. Cathy had wrapped herself in a blanket and was walking along still half asleep. I went to the kitchen phone and found the number of the Fire Department. They wanted to know how the fuel line got broken. Then I got the number of the heating company and phoned them. They asked if I'd phoned the firemen and then wanted to know how the fuel line got broken.

Cathy hadn't said anything, but she looked a bit frantic so Laura took her out to the car. Jacob offered to stay till the firemen and heating people came. We left him there and drove to my apartment. Almost every house we passed on the way had some kind of colored lights up. Even without snow everything looked nice, but I didn't think I'd mention that to Laura.

We got Cathy up to my apartment and I suggested that Laura make her some hot chocolate before she went to bed.

"Are we going to sleep here?" Cathy said.

Laura nodded.

"Just for tonight," she said.

When Laura went to the kitchen, Cathy sat in silence. I could see she was trying not to cry.

"Don't worry," I said. "We'll leave a note. Santa Claus will find you."

"I don't believe in Santa Claus," she said.

Laura came in with the hot chocolate.

"Cathy and you can have my big bed," I said. "Jacob can have the little bedroom, and I'll sleep here on the couch."

We didn't say anything while Cathy drank her chocolate,

and even when Laura had taken her off to the other room and put her in bed, we were silent, everything made strange by the child sleeping near us in a bed that was not her own. Still, I was happy in a way that we were there, ready to admit Jacob's wisdom, or maybe only one part of it, for I could see that Laura was worried and afraid that her house might be in flames. She kept fiddling with the back of her hair. I'd never seen her do that before.

"Do you want me to phone back to your place?" I said, "and see if everything's all right?"

"Would you mind? I'm pretty nervous."

I dialled her number. For a long time nobody answered, but finally Jacob came. He said everything was under control, that they had all the oil out of the basement, but that the fuel pipe wouldn't be fixed for a few hours at least.

I hung up and gave Laura the message.

"I'm sorry about this," I said. "Jacob always makes a little bit of chaos wherever he goes."

"In two weeks I'll laugh about it," Laura said. "Afterwards I'll think how refreshing it was, but right now I'm not sure I'm up to it." She reached out and took my hand.

I kissed her on the top of the head and went to put on a record.

"We'll have to go and get Cathy's presents," she said.

"Wait till Jacob gets back, then we'll go. We'll leave him to babysit."

"Do you think we'd dare?"

"I suppose not."

I sat down beside Laura on the couch. For an hour and a half we sat and waited for Jacob, and as we waited, we talked. It was strange, different from any other time. I even asked about her husband. Once or twice I called Laura's house looking for Jacob, but there was no answer. It was after eleven when the phone rang. It was Jacob.

"Where are you?" I said.

"At a police station."

"What in hell are you doing there?"

"They thought I was trying to steal a dog."

"What dog?"

"At the pound. I thought I'd get a dog for Cathy for Christmas."

"She doesn't want a dog."

"She'd love one. A great kid like that should have a dog, but when I went to the pound it was closed. I could hear dogs inside, and I figured if I could get one I could pay after the holidays. But when I climbed over the fence I got stuck and they saw me and now they won't let me explain."

"All right," I said. "I'll come." I found out where he was and hung up.

When I tried to explain to Laura, I started to giggle and then she started and I never got the whole story out. I wanted to keep Laura with me, so I got a teenager from down the hall to stay with Cathy and we drove to the police station.

The cops weren't too difficult about it. They hadn't charged him with anything, and one of them was a man I'd met a couple of times, a friend of a friend, so eventually we got Jacob out after I'd given my word that I'd keep him out of trouble. They thought he was just drunk.

As we drove home, everything started to seem unreal to me. I guess I was probably tired. I pulled into the parking lot and we all got out.

"Oh Jerry" Laura said, "I just remembered the presents."

"Back to the car," I said.

"It isn't far is it?" Jacob said. "We can walk. It will wake me up. You should always go out walking Christmas Eve."

I looked at Laura.

"It's a nice night," she said.

"Let's go," I said, and we started out. It was cold, but we

walked quickly and kept warm that way as we passed through the streets and parking lots that lay between my apartment and her house. Within a few minutes we were there.

We walked up the steps to the dark house and stood at the door while Laura looked for her key.

"Don't you have a key?" Jacob said to me.

"No."

Laura fumbled a little harder in her bag.

"Why not?" Jacob said.

"Here it is," she said. She got the door open. The house still smelled of oil, and it seemed as cold inside as out. Jacob beat his arms as he walked up and down the hall making a roaring noise. Laura stood at the door of the living room.

"I guess we'll just take the presents," she said.

"No," Jacob said, "we have to take the tree. We can't have Christmas without a tree."

"How can we take it?" I said.

Jacob looked at me. He was really surprised.

"Of course we can take it," he said. "We'll take off the decorations while Laura gets the presents packed."

I was too tired to argue. We began to take the decorations off. Jacob whistled happily, but I kept thinking that my eyes were going to close on me. Once or twice I stopped to watch Laura as she packed up the presents. It didn't take her long, and when she had finished, she sat down in a chair and closed her eyes. Sitting there, she looked small and old, vulnerable and desirable.

We had the tree stripped in a few minutes but had trouble getting the decorations packed away. I dropped a silver ball and broke it, then dropped another one.

"Out with you," Jacob said. "You take the tree and Laura take the presents and get on your way. I'll finish packing these and be right behind you."

"Okay," I said. I tried to pick up the tree and dropped it.

Tried again and got a face full of needles. Jacob manoeuvred me and the evergreen and got us in some kind of order. He pushed me out the door and helped Laura get the parcels settled in her arms.

"I'll be right along," he said.

Laura and I walked down the street and started across a parking lot. We didn't speak, just walked. The high buildings stood guard over our mad pilgrimage through the crackling cold, and above us a thousand stars gave their silent fire to the night. My face hurt from the scratching of spruce needles against my skin. Loaded down, we walked slowly, and there was no sound but the sound of our feet on the cold ground. Then, from behind us somewhere in that huge silence, came Jacob's voice, loud and raucous, but still a courageous noise in the face of winter, singing *O Come All Ye Faithful*. We stopped and listened.

"Laura," I said, "I don't agree with Cathy. I believe in Santa Clause. I can hear him singing to me."

She, my poor tired friend, tried to smile at me, or as much of me as she could see through the branches of that big spruce.

"Laura," I said, "I want to marry you."

In the distance I could still hear Jacob singing. Then I joined in.

Christmas at the Crompton

DAVID CAVANAGH

Violet pulled her old green blanket more tightly around her, bunched her pillow behind her back, lit another Rothmans, took a sip of 5-Star rye and water, and continued to look at the snow falling past the street lamp outside her window. She liked the snow: the way it moved so silently and the silence it gave the street below. She would not enjoy the uneven, slippery footing on the sidewalk after the snowfall, but she wasn't worried about that tonight. She didn't plan to go out until the day after tomorrow, when things would open again. It was Christmas Eve, and Violet was settled in.

She lived in the back corner room on the top floor of the Crompton Hotel, two storeys above the bar. Had lived there for nearly twelve years. Every day about noon she made the rounds of the hurricane deck, which was what her friend Nobby called their floor in the "good ship Crompton." Nobby lived in the front corner room with the curtain blowing out the window, even in winter, and as self-designated captain of the ship he alternately terrorized, delighted, and took care of "his crew" with his pranks, outlandish singing, and constant small favors. Next to Cootsy, who lived two doors down, Nobby was the youngest on the floor. He was sixty-two, but most people thought he looked eighty-nine and acted seven. No one was quite sure of Violet's age, though they all teased her unmercifully to try to find out. Violet would just ignore them when they got in moods like that, call them fools, and sip on her beer.

There were five others living on the hurricane deck: Don and Rickshaw (so named because he loved harness racing), Peep, Ralph, and old Al, who was so fat he rarely left his room because he found the steep wooden staircase such torture. Every day Violet would visit the rooms, starting with Nobby's, and would tidy up a little, change the beds when they needed it, and generally make sure everybody was all right. In this way she worked off her eighty-dollar-a-month rent.

Some days she wouldn't be feeling well: kind of wobbly and upset in her stomach. Still she would make her way down the hall to Nobby's room and knock on his door.

"Who is it?" he'd bellow, even though he knew her knock. When she didn't answer, he'd open the door and feign surprise. "Oh my God, it's Maid Marion, come in, come in," offering her his only chair, an old stuffed leather one with a curved metal frame and wooden armrests. Violet would carefully sit down, resting the pile of clean sheets in her lap.

"How was your trip through the woods, fair lady?" Nobby would croak in a voice that sounded like a bag of stones poured over a washboard. "Did you notice old Cootsy didn't make it back to his hole last night? Ho. Ho." When he said "Ho. Ho." which he did often, he breathed out each syllable distinctly, as if he were a diver getting ready to go under. "Maybe he got stuck in some other one. Pardon my Italian, fair damsel. So how are ya, old dear?"

"Not good today, Ian." Almost everybody called him Nobby, or Nob, maybe because his head was so bald and brown and tough, and as bold as a doorhandle. A few people called him "ya old buzzard," mostly with affection, though sometimes not. Only Violet called him Ian, his original name.

His voice would lower, "Well, don't worry about it, old sod. Just forget the beds for today. Twice a week's too often anyway." And they'd chat awhile, mostly about how the new owner of the hotel didn't treat them nearly as well as old Russ used to, but it didn't matter because "they'd outlast this new turk, the way he kept drinking up the profits of the bar." Then Violet would give Nobby a small smile and head back down the hall to the next room. Once she was inside and the door closed, Nobby would scuttle past and knock on all the other doors to tell the folks to take it easy on Violet, she wasn't feeling quite like the Queen Mother today.

Every night around midnight, after the rowdiest drinkers had gone away, Violet would come down to the bar, carefully sit at the little table near the front window, put her lighter and cigarettes on the table, and order two glasses of draft. Actually, she seldom had to order. The waiter would see her come in and bring her the beer. If Ned wasn't too drunk behind the bar, he would sometimes tell the waiter to say it was on the house. If he was in a mean mood, though, which was often, he would make some crack about the rooms she had cleaned that day, or didn't she think her liver was pickled enough already or some such thing. Violet wouldn't say a word but would light a cigarette, blow a long blue veil of smoke, and wait for her beer.

Usually, Nobby and Cootsy and a few others would join her and laugh and talk and sip beer. They never drank very much in the bar. Maybe they didn't want to be linked with the guzzlers who came in off the street. By closing time, one-thirty,

Violet would always be back upstairs in her room. She would have another small drink, settle into bed and think for a while until she fell asleep.

But tonight was Christmas Eve, and the bar had closed at six so the staff could be with their families. Violet decided to go to bed early, not to sleep but to watch the steady snowfall, which always got her thinking. Usually her thinking floated above the steady murmur that filtered up from the bar. She found the drone comforting. In the bar itself the sounds were sharper, like glasses clinking. The voices rose and fell individually, filled with laughter, anger, boredom, the stories Violet had heard and overheard, learned from and lived with for years. Sometimes she was deeply tired of what she saw there, but mostly she loved the bar.

For her, bars were the most honest places around. The true churches of Canada, as Nobby would say. People confessed their sins there and their dreams, revealed their blackest and most beautiful and most petty sides. She felt that they came to the hotel to do their worship: to pour out their hatred for this life, and their love of it, their meanness and kindness, their failures and what they wished could be. She laughed at how stupid they could be, how stupid she could be, and inside wanted to cry at how good they all wanted to be. And all of it shared over slim, cool glasses of golden communion. She had lived in many towns and cities, and in many ways, but she knew that she had settled down on the top floor of the Crompton because everything she had ever seen happened every night right below her in the bar. When it came right down to it, there was nowhere else to go.

But tonight there was no sound. The only people in the hotel were the eight of the them on this floor, the "permanents." Felt like Sunday, but different, too. Christmas Eve was always kind of strange. Silence on a Thursday night. Hard to get used to. At least the yeasty smell of beer, a hundred years of it, was still around. Incense. Hah. She took another sip of rye and thought that if the bar downstairs was the church, she and Nobby and Cootsy and the others must be — what? The statues? No, they moved around too much for that — must be the priests, and she must be a priestess. She liked that. She must remember to tell Nobby that one.

Her two-foot Christmas tree, plastic and gay with its little red lights and silver tinsel, winked at her from its spot on the high dresser that Ralph had painted white last month. Priests and priestess. And what a bunch of holy terrors. Lord, how they teased her. Cootsy's gift was staring at her right now from beside the tree: a small stuffed penguin wearing a floppy green shawl and a wig of tight little curls and with a Rothmans hanging out of its mouth. The gift had surprised her. She hadn't gotten out to get anything for any of them. Suddenly she felt sad at the way the snow was beginning to pile up on the sill outside her window. It was going by the street lamp on a sharp slant now, too fast. She decided to get out of bed.

After going to the bathroom down the hall, she found herself at the top of the stairs, looking down into the dimness lit only by the small red exit light on the next landing. Moving along beside the shiny rubbed railing, she made her way down into the bar.

The yellow glow behind the bar, the Molson sign and the large red exit sign over the street door provided the only light. The heavy round tables were like old men stooped in the shadows. She went to her usual table and sat down. In the dark. No TV, no voices, no sound of glasses being washed behind the bar. Christmas Eve. The windows were frosted. The storm seemed far away. She liked the quiet, but she also felt very empty and small in the dark corner. After a while she got up, went behind the bar and drew a glass of draft from the spigot. She could hardly reach it, but by hoisting herself a little with her elbow on the counter she managed. She walked carefully with the full glass back to her table, lit a cigarette, and took a sip of beer.

Her Christmas Eve party. A bar to herself. Stolen beer tasted good. If Ned ever saw her he'd wet his pants. Would suit him just fine, she thought, the big horse. The eight-foot tinfoil Merry Christmas over the bar made her laugh. She drained her glass and got up. This time she brought back two draft, her usual. "Thank you, Ned, bring them right over here. My table, Ned." She put a quarter tip on the table. "Next time take away the empties, Ned, or we'll find someone who will." She laughed a little. God, Violet, what are you doing stealing beer and talking to the air? "Merry Christmas, Violet," she toasted out loud and drained the glass.

A few minutes later she got up for two more draft, and a few minutes after that, two more. It began to be difficult to make the trip from the bar to her table, but she was damned if she would sit behind the bar on Ned's stool and slop down beer. She moved slowly back to her table, spilling some as she stepped down the one step between her table and the bar. "Damn." Lit another cigarette. Choked a bit, and took a big swallow of beer. She knew she was getting drunk. Knew she should be back in her room. Knew her room was the only place she was safe when she was like this. They'd laugh at her. She didn't mind the teasing of the bunch upstairs — they were like her, no better and in some ways worse off — but she wouldn't stand for anyone in the bar laughing at her. Ned laughing at her. The stuffed hog. She started to cry, the tears wetting her hand wrapped around the beer glass. The wrinkles. How did they ever get so wrinkled, she thought. Damn. Ned, you bugger. And knew that she was not just talking to Ned. He was just like her son — huge belly, mean, big voice — who lived in Edmonton now. Hadn't talked to her for over eight years. Owned three trucks last time she'd heard. Made her cry to see how he hated his kids, his wife, her, the way he talked about racing the bohunks on the highway, the way he talked about her. Ned. Just like him. She got up. Got two more glasses of draft and a shot of rye from the bottles kept under the counter and put them all on a tray. Made it back to the table but knocked some of the empties on the floor as she put down the tray. She was crying hard now. "I'll clean it up, Ned. Damn you, I'll clean it."

"Oh my God, it's Mother Superior."

It was Nobby, standing in the doorway leading from the staircase, light from the Molson Golden sign glinting off his head. "Thought I heard something. What the devil are you doing down here on the poop deck?" When he saw her face, he just came over and sat down. He took her left hand. That surprised both of them. "Don't worry, Violet. It isn't worth it."

"I know, but sometimes I can't help it."

"I know, I know." Nobby leaned down and picked up the fallen glasses. He didn't ask what was wrong. It was the same with him some days. "What are you trying to do, make me work all through the birth of Our Lord?" It was Nobby's job to clean up the bar every morning before it opened. "Can I buy you a drink, Rapunzel?" Violet tried to grin and pointed to the empties on the table. Nobby moved behind the bar and brought back a trayful of beer. "Quite an idea you've got here. Don't move. I'll be right back."

He went to the bottom of the stairway and hollered Cootsy's name like a volley of cannon shots. Cootsy's head finally appeared at the top of the stairs.

"Ah, there you are. Alert the bridge, dear Coots. The Queen of Sheba's down here, and she's inviting everyone to a party on the poop. Ho. Ho. Tell them all to bring their stomachs and their dancing shoes."

It wasn't long before they all trooped down: Ralph, and Don, and Peep, and Rickshaw, carrying a transistor, and Cootsy, shaking his head and grinning like a chimp. "Oh Nobby, you've done it this time. Let's do it real Merry, 'cause we're gonna need a new home in the New Year."

"Never mind that, Cootsy old son, pass around some of this beer." And he handed him another trayful.

They were all awed by what was happening. All of them had, in one way or other, lived on the fringes of society for years, were used to being outcasts, even enjoyed it when things were going well: when their veterans' and old age pensions came in, when Cootsy got a raise at Canadian Tire, when Rickshaw won at the track, or when they staged one of their frequent and complicated pranks, such as the day they moved all of Al's furniture into the big bathroom and stuffed his room from floor to ceiling with balled newspaper while he was out. They were used to themselves and to their lives, difficult or strange as they sometimes seemed, even to them, but they still relied on their routines, and they knew the boundaries that their outrageousness had to live within. They knew now that they were going beyond these bounds, drinking Ned's beer in his closed-up bar on Christmas Eve.

It made them hesitant at first, but also giddy. Soon they were hooting and drinking and telling old stories that had them in tears. Even old Al finally lumbered down the stairs to see what the commotion was about and in no time was holding forth, his mammoth rear spread across two chairs, about the time they flew Violet's underwear from the top of the TV antenna on the roof of the hotel. The flag of the good ships Lolly and Poop, Nobby called it at the time.

Rickshaw turned on the radio, and amid more trips to the bar they started dancing. Violet refused to dance but was tapping her feet and smiling through her cigarette smoke. Nobby told her she had beautiful hands, and kissed one of them. She shoved him away and shook her head at him the way she always did. Peep did a Spanish sword dance on the bar while they all clapped, and Nobby kept hopping all over the room, handing out beer and booming out, "Ho. Ho. Who has more fun than the poor people? Press on, press on, Lancelot." This last to Ralph, who was galloping toward the dartboard with Al's cane thrust out in front of him.

Everything would probably have been fine if Cootsy hadn't asked old fat Al to dance with him, and if Nobby and Cootsy and Rickshaw hadn't hauled Al to his feet against his protests. Soon Cootsy and Al were blimping around the room like a balloon blown up, turned loose and gone crazy, only in slow motion. Nothing was safe. Four hundred pounds of drunken enthusiasm knocked over tables, chairs, Nobby, just missed the color television, and finally fell against the crossbar handle of the street door.

Two things happened simultaneously. One was that Cootsy and Al disappeared from sight into the street. The other was that a shrill bell started clanging loud enough that even Violet stood up and stared, frozen with the others, at the once again closed door. It was the burglar alarm.

"Oh my God, we must be on fire. Abandon ship!" hollered Nobby and jumped behind the bar to find the switch to turn off the alarm. The bell clanged on and on. Most of the others were holding their ears and yelling at Nobby to hurry up and find the goddamn switch. Finally it stopped. They all looked at each other, wondering what next.

They didn't have to wait long. Cootsy and Al burst back into the bar, Al swearing himself hoarse and heading for a couple of chairs and Cootsy burbling and mumbling in a mixture of laughter and fear. It seemed a police car was heading their way down the main drag, red lights flashing. Cootsy had thought for a minute it was a Christmas tree coming to see what happened. Just then they heard the car pull up to the curb outside the door.

"Oh my God, the Gestapo," whispered Nobby and headed for the door. "This is it, mates. See you in el hoosegow." And then, "Violet, quick. Go on upstairs."

Violet just sat down, pulled her shawl around her, took another sip of beer and reached for a cigarette. "Best party I've been to in years," she said, and waved him towards the door.

There was a knock, and Nobby called out, "Who is it?"

"Police. Who are YOU?"

Nobby opened the door and was greeted by the glare of a flashlight shone directly into his eyes. "Come in, gentlemen, come in, I didn't realize it was already noon."

Two large policemen, made larger by their winter parkas, came into the room and flashed their lights at Don and Ralph and Al and Peep and Cootsy and Rickshaw and the overturned chairs and tables and finally at Violet, sitting calmly smoking at her table in the corner. It was nearing midnight on Christmas Eve in a bar that had closed six hours ago, and there were about twenty empty and half-empty beer glasses on her table alone. "Hello, George, Paul. Won't you sit down?" She waved to two upright chairs at the next table.

Ralph pretended to faint over by the bar. Nobby just grabbed his head in both hands and looked on.

"What the hell's going on here, Violet?" the policeman called George said. So Violet explained. How she'd been up in her room, how she'd got feeling blue, since it was Christmas Eve, how she'd come down, how Nobby had heard her and come to help her out, how they'd all decided to have a party to cheer her up, and how things got a wee bit too merry, and how the door had tripped the alarm. It was quite a long story, and the two policemen just listened quietly.

When Violet was finished, the one called Paul said, "Does Ned Tanner know you're in here tonight?"

"I wouldn't think so," Violet said, and took a sip of beer.

Silence. And then finally Paul said, "Well, George, do you

see any damage or signs of a break-in?"

"Nope," said George, "no sign of a break-in. Somebody better check that alarm. Must've shorted out."

"Guess so. Well, folks, too bad you have to work on Christmas Eve cleaning up the bar. Ned's kind of a mean bugger to make you work tonight. Hope it doesn't take too long. Have a good Christmas."

And they left.

"Oh my God, Mary Magdalene, you're a real Christmas bonus!" croaked Nobby, shaking his head.

Violet just raised her glass and smiled. "Who has more fun than the poor people, eh Nobby?"

The Surrogates

BEATRICE FINES

The little radio on the bedside table said "blizzard warning," but the few white motes dancing down the face of the red brick building across the street didn't look like trouble to Henry. He turned away from the window and crossed the narrow hotel room to the wash basin in the corner, rubbing his hand over the rough stubble of his jaw. Barry would expect him to be clean-shaven and spruced up.

The blade in the BIC throw-away was dull and his face was stinging when he finished his shave. He drew his fingers across his cheeks. Good firm flesh there, no wrinkles, just a few lines around his eyes. Those came from working outside all his life. He dipped his comb in the water wishing he had some greasy stuff for his hair. Never would lie flat, always had that rooster comb at the back, but thick, thick as a bear's coat in winter. Barry had his mother's hair, soft as a kitten's fur, yellow as a dandelion when he was little. Thirty years since they left — thirty years or yesterday.

Henry pulled on his best pants, the ones without grease or holes from battery acid. Plaid shirt, plaid mackinaw, peaked cap. Respectable enough. Barry wouldn't expect to see him in a three-piece suit. He'd get the kid a room at the Marlborough. This second-rate Winnipeg hotel was okay for him but Barry was probably used to more class. Maybe they'd eat at the Marlborough too. The boss said they put up a good feed on Christmas day. Did you have to wear a tie there? Maybe he should buy a white shirt, one of those dress shirts and a tie.

The snowflakes were scudding sideways across the circle of light from the street lamp below his window now, and the sky had disappeared.

"The storm warning continues," said the radio. "The temperature has dropped ten degrees to minus fourteen celsius and the wind velocity has increased to between 35 and 40 kilometres an hour."

Celsius, kilometers, what the hell did that mean?

"West bound travel is not advised. Visibility on the Trans-Canada is half a kilometer in snow and blowing snow."

So it was thickening up, but it couldn't be that bad. Hell, how'd they like to cross a lake in a white-out when the sky and the earth were both swallowed up, using nothing but their instincts and the direction of the wind? He'd done it many times, sitting high in the frigid cab of an out-moded snow-plough.

The tall buildings poured wind at him from every direction of the compass when Henry set off for the bus depot half a mile away. Out in the country the wind was honest. Overhead, metal arches hung with star and flower shapes outlined with red, green, and yellow lights were so pretty it was almost worth the trip just to see them. Still, city life was not for him. After a few days the rush, the crowds, the noise, so filled his head there was no room for figuring things out.

Inside the depot the air was thick with the smell of stale

smoke, rubber boots, pinesol, and cooking oil from the cafeteria next to the waiting room. Henry leaned back against the bench and folded his hands across his stomach, aware that the security guard was eyeing him. It was his fourth visit to the depot that week. To-night the place was almost empty. Two old biddies in fur coats were staring at the arrivals board, pointing to it and looking at each other nervously. Two middle-aged Indian women in short, bulky jackets and pants that bulged over sagging bellies whispered in a corner. A young man in an army surplus jacket went into the cafeteria, his boots impatiently loud on the tile floor.

Five-forty-five and no arrivals. Six-fifteen and still no buses. Henry got up and went to the door. The storm could no longer be denied. The street lamps were haloed and distant behind thick veils, and long fingers of snow had formed across the parking lot. But a bus was coming in at last. Henry watched as the driver alighted. But this was not Barry. This man was dark, tall, loose-limbed. Barry would be fair-skinned with a solid, broad-shouldered body. He was sure of that.

For ten minutes the depot was like a pot brought suddenly to a boil, bubbling with sound and movement. Henry stopped a middle-aged man who was alone, unencumbered by chattering relatives or friends.

"Pardon me, but where was this bus from?"

"Thunder Bay," said the man, pushing past him.

There might still be a bus from Saskatoon then. In a few minutes only the security guard and a young couple with a baby remained in the waiting room, and the depot echoed with distant, hollow sounds. The young man was at the telephone, holding the receiver to his ear and biting his lip. The girl, with the sleeping baby in her lap, watched him, her face tight and anxious.

"No answer," the man said.

Henry edged closer, hungry for the sound of their voices.

The only words he'd spoken to another human being in four days were brief good mornings to the clerk in the hotel.

"We were late. They should be here by now," the girl answered.

Henry seized the opportunity the storm gave him. "Pardon me, but what's it like out in the country?"

They turned to him. "Pretty bad, the last forty miles. I guess it's worse further west," the man said.

Henry felt his face muscles sag.

"Are you expecting someone from the west?" the girl asked solicitously.

"Yes. My son. But then, I've seen buses come in one, two, even three hours late. You folks, now, you headed west?"

The girl shifted the sleeping baby. "No. My parents were to meet us. They farm thirty miles north of the city."

A small frown appeared between her eyebrows. Mary'd had eyebrows like that, curved like a gull's wing.

"We're afraid they're stuck on the road someplace."

"We can go to a hotel if they don't get in," said the young man looking down at his wife and coaxing a smile to his lips.

"Not the best way to spend Christmas," said the girl, bending her head over the baby.

The young man went back to the phone, dialled, listened, and finally hung up, shaking his head. The baby had wakened and now began to fuss, rubbing a small fist around its mouth.

"Is he hungry?" Henry asked.

"She. And I expect she is." The girl smiled. She had good even teeth.

She handed the baby to her husband and fumbled around in the large carry-all at her feet, finally producing a feeding bottle.

"Hard traveling with a baby," said Henry. "Once when my son was small, we got stuck while driving to Winnipeg and it was twenty below."

You and Barry alone in that thick dark, that country dark. You never forgave me for that, did you Mary?

"What happened?"

"Oh, I got to a farm a mile or so down the road and the farmer came and pulled us out with his team. No harm done, no harm done."

Where was the harm? Was it the bush, the cold, and the distances, or was it me? The hydro did come, you know, and a paved road. If you'd waited a year, maybe two. . .

"My son was about his — her — size when that happened, but he was all right. My wife, her name was Mary — she was able to keep the truck running for heat. I always kept the tank topped up in winter."

"Of course," said the young man. He handed the baby back to his wife and sat down beside her. "We'll wait until she's fed and I'll try the phone once more before we look for a hotel," he said, smiling down at the child who had begun to suck noisily.

Henry went to the door and looked out. The snow was now a heavy swirling curtain. He glanced back at the little family, mother, father, and child.

"Say," he said, speaking too loudly to quiet the tremor in his voice, "would you folks have some supper with me while you wait?" He moved towards them awkwardly. "I'd sure enjoy the company."

The girl glanced at her husband who smiled first at her and then at Henry. "I guess we can do that," he said.

Henry's heart was hammering as he led the way to the cafeteria.

There was an embarrassing exchange once they had reached the cashier's desk after picking up their food (hamburgers, coleslaw, and fries). Henry, first in line, pulled out his wallet with a flourish.

"These three," he said importantly.

"No, no," the young man protested, drawing his own wallet from his pocket.

"Please let me. I insist," said Henry.

"Oh we shouldn't really . . ." The girl looked distressed.

"Ah, make an old man happy," said Henry, holding out two twenties, chagrined when gently reminded that one was enough. Only when he had his guests securely ensconced in the plastic upholstered booth (the baby in a high chair at the end) did the trembling in his knees ease.

"My name's Henry, by the way," he said. "Henry Boulanger."

They said they were Pat and Allan Andrews. The baby was amanda. She was seven months old and her grandparents had only seen her once.

"Did you say it was your son you were expecting?" Allan asked.

"Yes. He's about your age."

"Married?"

Was he? And was there a child like this child back there in Saskatoon?

"We've been . . . out of touch."

Thirty years. Pride kept me from going after you, Mary, and then you left the city and I had no idea where you'd gone.

The young man and his wife were looking at him with tender eyes. Henry felt the tight muscles around his stomach loosen.

"I just found out where my boy was lately, sort of by accident, and I sent him a letter. I'm not one for writing letters, but I did it and he sent a card back."

It was in his pocket, a somewhat crumpled postcard with a picture of the Banff Springs Hotel and a few lines of print script on the back.

Thanks for the letter. I'll be doing the Saskatoon-Winnipeg run once or twice during Christmas week while the regular guys are taking time off. It will be the first I've been back there since I was a kid.

Henry looked up and saw something in the faces across the table that loosed a stream of words from the cataract of his mind.

"His mother and I separated years ago, you see. Water under the bridge, water under the bridge. My boy drives for Greyhound and he's doing the Saskatoon-Winnipeg run this week, so I took the chance to come into the city . . . but he hasn't come yet. I figured it would be to-night for sure. Unless the storm . . . and day after to-morrow I got to get back home. I only got the week off. I work on the roads, driving snowploughs in winter, graders in summer. Keeps me fit, being outside in all kinds of weather, I even plough winter roads across the ice on the lakes. That's when you have to keep your head on straight. My wife . . ."

Always afraid, weren't you Mary, for yourself and for me.

"My wife was from England — near London. We got married over there in forty-five. I was in the army. She was excited about coming to Canada, but . . ."

It was not as you imagined it, was it Mary? The little old house in the center of those stoney fields and all that poplar bush. None of those little fields and hedges with the neighbors and the village pub a five-minute walk away and the green grocer calling by every morning. I tried to explain how it was over here but the pictures in your mind didn't change, did they?

"I got a little farm through the VLA, the Veteran's Land Act, you know, east of here. I was going in for cattle and I was going to build a new house on the place but those things take time. Took a lot of money to get started in cattle even in them days. You know anything about farming?"

Allan shook his head. "I work in the city — Thunder Bay."

"Yeah. Well, I went into the bush cutting pulpwood and hauling it to the mill at Pine Falls. Had to do it, you know. It was a hard life in the bush camps those years. Today they got trailers all hooked up to the electric or with propane, but we were in log bunkhouses where you could freeze your tail off."

Henry shook his head, remembering. Gad the smells of the place! Sweaty wool socks steaming on the clothes lines behind the heater and tobacco smoke a blue cloud between floor and ceiling. He could see Corky and the Swede and old Ollie slapping the greasy cards down on the table playing poker and the freckled kid from Lac du Bonnet squatting in the corner, squeaking out a tune on his harmonica.

We couldn't keep the lice and the bedbugs down, Mary, but I threw my long johns away before I came home. I don't know how the blasted things got into the house.

"You must have worked hard," Pat encouraged and Henry raised his voice to meet the challenge of an audience.

"Well, I was tough in them days. And I like the bush. All kinds of things to see and peaceful like. I mind one time I was resting a bit beside a big pile of pulpwood. Nice day, it was, with the sky bluer than you'd believe and fresh snow, all sparkly, and not a whisper of wind. I must have dozed a little, being comfortable, my back against the woodpile, and I woke up and there was this bull moose looking at me from over the top with that long ugly muzzle just inches from my face."

Henry laughed, relishing the amazement on the faces across the table. "I scrambled onto my hands and knees, my hands and knees, by God, and crawled some before I stood up and when

I looked back he was still there, looking at me. Then he turned and ambled off, so slow, slow. I swear he was laughing at me. I swear he was tickled with himself for scaring me."

Henry stared at the wall. What would Barry say if he told him that story?

"Imagine that!" Pat's voice roused him.

"Yeah. We got a lot of game around the camp. My wife — Mary didn't care for it a lot. Never eaten it before, you see. Very fond of seafood, she was, and other things she'd been used to in England. Always planned on scraping up enough money so she could go back for a visit but you know how it is. I never was out of a job, though. Worked the camps, then the roads. Built muscles I ain't never lost. Hard work never hurt a man."

Killed your spirit though, didn't it Mary. Pumping water, feeding calves and all the rest when I was away.

"It was hard on my wife, me being away so much, but what could I do? Farm wasn't paying much and there was the boy growing up. When he was six she said we should move to town for his schooling. Wanted me to sell the farm. But I was just getting it going by then. Haven't got it now though. Gave it up ten years ago."

Henry's throat thickened.

"I couldn't blame her for going. She got a job here in the city. For a couple of years I thought . . . I got the hydro in and I thought . . . but she had this other guy by then. Ah, I shouldn't be bothering you with all this. Lots of water under the bridge since then anyway."

Henry slapped his palm against the table. "I've had a good life. Done the work I wanted to do and got respect. My boss now, he brags about me and I make pretty good money. I got no worries, no worries at all."

"That's good. Not many people can say that," said Allan.

Henry let the silence build for a minute before he went on. "Did I tell you how I found my boy? Boss went to Saskatoon looking to buy a re-conditioned grader and then he took the bus to Regina and there was my Barry, driving. The name was posted up front and it struck him and he said 'I got a fellow named Boulanger with a son named Barry working for me' and sure enough, it was my Barry. I was hoping to see him, but . . ."

Henry stared over the heads of his guests. "Leastways I know where he is now. Maybe I'll go up there. To Saskatoon. I never been to Saskatoon."

The meal was over. Allan pushed his empty plate aside and Pat laid her knife and fork carefully across hers. Then Allan stood up. "I'll try once more," he said, nodding towards the waiting room and the telephone.

"I'll carry the baby," Henry offered and took the child in awkward arms. The soft warmth of the small body flooded his mind and he stood for a moment, swaying a little.

"I'm sorry Henry, but I just can't continue living this kind of life."

Mary's letter propped against the lamp on the kitchen table, and the empty echo of his own footsteps as he walked through the house, room by room, until he had to believe, not to accept, never to accept, but to believe. He tightened his hold on the baby, feeling the pain of a parting that was years old and as new as this minute.

Allan was already talking on the phone, nodding and smiling. Joining thumb and forefinger he signalled his wife.

"They're home. They got as far as Stonewall and had to turn back. If the plough goes through they'll come in the morning."

Pat reached out a hand. "Let me talk."

As her voice lifted and lightened with relief, Henry's throat grew tighter. When she had finished and held out her arms for the baby, he had to turn his face aside.

"Thanks, Mr. Boulanger," she said and he nodded dumbly and followed her to the door.

Traffic was moving slowly on the snow-rutted street. A solitary cab stood at the taxi stand. Allan and Pat turned bright faces to Henry before getting in.

"Thanks again for supper," Allan said, "and if we don't get out to the farm tomorrow may we phone you and take you to dinner?"

Henry straightened his shoulders. "That would be nice, very nice, but my son might be here by then. You never know."

"Where are you staying?" Allan asked.

Henry looked at his feet. "Oh me, I'm not one for fancy places." He named the hotel. "I just bunk in there when I come to the city, but when my son comes we'll go to the Marlborough."

"Well we'll try to get in touch in the morning," said Allan.

"I'll keep in touch."

Those had been the last words on Mary's long ago note.

Something Special

JOYCE MITCHELL

The sun winked then sobered as it fought a losing battle to the wind pushing it's gray, snow-laden burden across the sun's vanishing face. It was early afternoon as the three in the car headed east from the city to the tree cutting area. The boy, bundled warmly, was fidgeting restlessly between them. The young mother peeled off the outer layers and pulled off his overboots. Her husband was singing *Jingle Bells* loudly, tapping his fingers on the steering wheel and making faces at the boy who was soon clapping his hands and singing along as best a four-year-old can. She leaned back, dreamily contented, feeling safe and happy in her world, which was the three of them. She could picture the decorated tree in front of the living room window. To her it looked nicer than the one on the cover of Eaton's Christmas catalogue or in *Chatelaine*. It was perfectly symmetrical. Perched at the very top on a long slender branch was a golden angel with her billowing robe of scarlet, green, gold, and silver that winked seductively when anyone came near. She laughed to herself. How foolish. But this would be their first Christmas in their very own, tiny new home and she wanted everything to be perfect.

Abruptly, the droning of snowmobiles, the roaring of cars rocking backward and forward to be free of ever deepening ruts, and loud, excited voices jarred her from her reverie. They had arrived.

Following in phantom footsteps, the boy frequently fell, laughing into the fluffy down. Once, helping him up, they gave in to temptation, abandoning their pursuit for the moment and, like school kids once again, made angels in the snow.

The first topped tree was a disappointment. It had gaping holes down one side.

"Okay," he said, "you pick the next one."

She gazed up at the tall spruce. From down here they all looked the same but she had to choose. This one too was a disappointment.

"Let's try once more," she said uneasily, glancing nervously at her son. They had been out for almost two hours and she was beginning to feel the cold.

The third one was short and stubby, not at all what she wanted but they kept it. The ride home was in sharp contrast to the previous one. The boy lay sleeping across her lap. She could feel her husband's tenseness, his eyes on the road, his fingers gripping the steering wheel. She knew he was frustrated with her because she wasn't happy with their tree. She told him it was fine but he knew.

She sighed, leaning back trying to relax but she couldn't. Thoughts of Christmases past came to her. Although life with a father who drank not infrequently was difficult, Christmas was always very special. Then she remembered the Christmas when she was eleven.

It was late afternoon of Christmas eve. She and her older brother had just walked the two miles from town. They were excited because their father had given them ten dollars to spend on presents and they were eager to wrap them. As they entered the house they saw their four younger siblings at the table with crayons and coloring books. Their mother was busy with steaming pots and pans at the wood burning cookstove. She did not look up. They looked around the crowded room then quizzically at each other.

"Where's the tree Mom?" he asked.

"There won't be a tree this year, John, there's no room."

"There won't be a tree? But we've always had a tree. It won't be Christmas without one."

"I'm sorry," she said in a tired voice, "but this year, moving to this tiny place because of your father's drinking, there's just no room."

The defeated sound of her mother's voice made her feel uneasy. Mother had never mentioned their father's drinking to them before. It was something that they had learned to live with and never discussed. Always her mother had taken such pride in her tree and decorated it herself. The children were allowed to unwrap and hand her the ornaments as she carefully hung each one. This ritual was usually performed the day before Christmas eve. There was such a warmth, a family closeness that was so special at Christmas. She thought perhaps it was so special because it was the only time her father never drank. They always had lots of presents and her mother cooked along with a turkey, a big, fat goose, which her father preferred. For dessert there were apple and pumpkin pies and lots of plump, steamed plum pudding, its cloth casing tied with string. Sitting ripening since early November in a crock container were three square fruit cakes.

Suddenly she felt drained. To be in such a high state of excitement and now this left her with a strange emptiness she had never felt before. She knew her brother must feel the same. She looked at him. Instinctively each knew what the other was thinking as they grabbed their mitts and scarves and headed out into the falling snow.

Already the little light remaining was fading fast. They sprinted down the wide path along the river which led to a dense stand of spruce about a quarter mile away. They reached it quickly and searched in vain for a small tree. Not finding one, they then tried to chop down one of the bigger trees. Having in their haste grabbed an axe but not a saw, it was a useless effort for it was already dark and they would still have to top it. They hadn't realized till now how big and tough these trees were. They decided to search the scrub between the riverpath and the road to town, it being less dense, they had a better chance of spotting their prize. They walked briskly, eyes scanning the darkness but still could see no spruce. How could this be? This was their haunt. They knew every blade of grass, every stump, how could they not know there were no small spruce? There were poplars, oaks, and maples. There were cranberry, chokecherry, and wild plum but not a spruce could they find. She remembered the expression about people not seeing the forest for the trees, but she and her brother it seemed couldn't see the trees for the forest.

They were both cold and hungry now but they wouldn't give in. The sky had begun to clear and stars blinked here and there between the shifting clouds. She knew by the stinging warmth of her toes that they were frozen.

"Maybe we should take this dogwood," John said hopefully. "It would look nice decorated. Just in case we don't find a spruce on our way back." She knew he was frozen too. She answered listlessly that it would be better than nothing. As John began swinging the axe, she thought she'd take one last look around before they headed for home. Suddenly she started jumping up and down, squealing and jabbering incoherently from excitement and the cold for she had spotted a spindly lone spruce five feet away.

She no longer felt cold nor hunger as they hurried home with their scraggly, precious prize. They could see their mother's anxious face in the light of the doorway as her eyes searched the darkness in the direction of the exuberant chatter.

"Mama, Mama, look what we've got — a tree, a Christmas tree!" they shouted deliriously in unison.

Their mother made them eat big bowls of soup, rubbing their feet as they ate, promising them she would help set the tree up on her Singer in the front window as soon as they finished eating. She insisted they decorate it as she handed them the ornaments. She would never forget the look on her mother's face as the three of them decorated it together. But the thing she treasured most about that Christmas was not the smile on her mother's lips; it was the smile in her mother's eyes as she bustled about the tree.

They were nearing the city. She touched her husband's arm.

"Tonight, while we're decorating our tree, I'll tell you a story," she said.

Christmas Temptation

HAYDN BRISLEY

"I shall consider I have been slighted if you refuse." Owen Bradshaw, President and General Manager of Bradshaw and Smythe, pronounced the words in his usual manner — pompous, autocratic and without seeming regard for any prior needs or wishes of his audience. His glance back at Anstruther was hard and penetrating. "Greatly slighted, Anstruther . . . Take the remainder of the day off and go pack a change of clothing . . . Dinner will be at nine." He let the door slam behind him.

George Anstruther stilled his shaking hands and wiped his palms on the handkerchief from his breast pocket. Why in Heaven's name would the old man want him to spend the Christmas at Bradshaw Villa? A forty room mausoleum which the Bradshaw clan called home. Thirty years he had worked for the company and he had never heard of anyone being invited there before. He nervously tidied his desk, put reference books away, and flipped the cassette from his dictating machine.

Hoots of laughter and the strident sounds of noise makers came from the offices on the lower floor.

"Anstruther," he answered, as the intercom phone rang.

"Will you be down to see the staff before they leave today Mister Anstruther? You know, being Christmas Eve and all that."

Anstruther recognized the voice as that of his assistant who was young, upwardly mobile, ambitious enough to have reached the third highest position in the company at the age of thirty four — yet not smart enough to realize he was under paid.

"Yes, Thornby, I shall be leaving soon — I'll drop in on the way through."

"Okay, Sir, see you then."

With the peremptory summons to attend Bradshaw Villa still on his mind, Anstruther was slow to replace the phone set. Through the earpiece, thin but plainly audible came Thornby's voice. "This may be old George's last official duty . . . There's a rumor he . . . " The phone went dead as Thornby hung up.

Anstruther stood transfixed. What had he just heard? A rumor that he would not be around much longer. Suddenly the summons to the President's home for the holidays made some sense. He was being given the golden handshake. Forced into early retirement so that some whippersnapper could be put in his place at half the pay.

He walked to the small toilet-cum-wash-area and rinsed his face with a cold cloth. He was still drying off when he heard the office door open.

"He's already left." It was Bradshaw's voice.

"Good. How did you get him to agree to come? Did you tell him, Owen?"

Anstruther had met Mrs. Bradshaw on the most casual basis, but her voice was unmistakable.

"No, I didn't tell him . . . I more or less leaned on him a bit

". . . Perhaps for the last time."

The two speakers were out of the office now and walking along the hallway; Anstruther ran to the door and opened it a crack. They were getting into the elevator.

"Are you sure that young man can handle the job?"

"Of course he can . . . with the right influence." The doors closed on the remainder of Bradshaw's reply.

The afternoon was a blur to George Anstruther. He expressed best wishes of the management to the assembled staff, accepted handshakes in return, and arrived home at his service apartment without being able to remember anyone he had spoken to at the office party.

Why now? he reflected. When I need the job so much. He thought of Betty, his wife of twenty years, who had passed away the previous year. The demanding work at Bradshaw and Smythe had been his salvation from maudlin obscurity after her death. He smiled grimly as he poured a three finger scotch. He had never been intoxicated in his fifty two years — what would they think if he turned up smashed?

Soon after seven, Anstruther left his car with a footman and presented his hat and coat to the butler. He was told that his overnight bag would be put in his room as soon as the footman had put the car away. The butler was a snob; he delegated the duty of showing Anstruther to his room to a maid, new to the job. "Mr. Bradshaw says that you should make yourself comfortable. There will be people assembling for drinks in the library and he will see everyone at dinner." She paused at the door. "Dinner will be at nine sharp."

The effect of the large scotch had passed, leaving a dull throb in his temples. He succumbed to temptation and flopped on the bed for a few moments while he stared at the ceiling. Thoughts flitted through his mind as he reviewed thirty years with Bradshaw and Smythe. Thirty years of hard work, scrupulous honesty, and unstinted self sacrifice. He remembered, without rancor, the missed holidays when company duty called; his wife's distress at trips taken alone. He drifted quietly into sleep.

He awoke with a peculiar vibration in his ears and a sense of disorientation. There was a rap on the door.

"George? George Anstruther. Are you in there?"

"Come in, it's open," Anstruther struggled to a sitting position on the edge of the bed, trying to place the voice.

"Holy cow, you're not dressed yet — the gong's gone for dinner."

Anstruther looked with displeasure at his assistant Thornby. Thornby had never called him by his first name before. Was this an indication?

"I didn't know you were invited here Thornby. You didn't say anything this afternoon."

"I didn't know then George. Say, you'd better hurry or you will get the old man teed off."

"Yes, yes," agreed Anstruther testily. "Get out of here and I'll get changed and be right down."

"Right O. See you." As Thornby closed the door, something fell. George walked across the room and picked up the handkerchief Thornby had dropped.

"Young upstart, taking on airs. Monogrammed handkerchief indeed," he muttered to himself as he stuffed the offending linen into the pocket of his dressing gown and moved hastily to the bathroom.

The guests were already seated when George arrived; he would have liked to slip quietly into a chair, but the butler made a great show of leading him to a seat near the head of the table while the talk slowly dwindled to a mutter.

"Well George, I'll bet this is the first time you have been late since you became associated with Bradshaw & Smythe. Eh! What! Bad example for young Thornby here." Bradshaw shot a sardonic glance at Thornby, who was already seated, resplendent in tails.

Anstruther smiled thinly. Suddenly it didn't matter any more. If they wanted him out they were going to have to push; he wouldn't oblige them by walking away.

"My apologies to yourself and your lovely wife, Sir," Anstruther said, and turned to the young woman sitting at his left to engage her in conversation. Around the table the murmur of voices rose again.

The food was exceptional, the company capable of carrying on an intelligent conversation, the Christmas toasts witty and short, and George Anstruther found he was enjoying himself. He smiled inwardly when he caught either of the Bradshaws watching him. Because he felt that there was little he could do to worsen his situation, he relaxed, adding to the banter about the table, displaying a sense of humor never suspected by his fellow workers.

It was late when the dinner party broke up. Bradshaw had one last directive: "Sleep in if you wish, ladies and gentlemen, but my wife and I would appreciate your attendance at the Christmas tree by eleven." He regarded the guests benignly. "There will be a little something for everyone. Eh! So let's not have any stragglers . . . Eh, George?"

The group broke up, laughing and chattering. George went to his room, his few hours of carefree enjoyment ripped away by sudden doubts. It would happen at the tree tomorrow; he would be handed something of value and told that his services were no longer required — farmed out to retirement.

In pyjamas and slippers, George prowled his room and bath. On a side table, bottles of scotch and rye had been left, together with suitable mixers and a bucket of ice. George helped himself to a large scotch and lay down. Two hours and four drinks later he was still awake. Perhaps a book would help.

He crept along the hall; all sounds of movement had ceased.

Servants away to well earned rest, guests to their own, or someone else's bed.

At the bottom of the stairs he had a choice of several rooms. Entering one at random, he found himself in the study. He was about to leave when he noticed the bright jacketed novels on the desk — some McDonalds, a Follett, several Ludlums. He picked one he had not read and once again started to leave, when he saw the open safe. He stepped closer – it did not look as though it had been forced, it had probably been left open.

He tucked his book selection in his dressing gown pocket and his fingers touched the handkerchief — Thornby's handkerchief. The plan to hurt Thornby came to him instantly and in full bloom. What would Bradshaw think when next he opened his safe . . . when he found Thornby's handkerchief inside? No sooner the plan than the deed. He tossed the damning linen in the safe and shut the door. As he walked past the desk on the way out, his steps slowed.

"Goddammitt, I can't do it," he gave a short, bitter laugh. "I guess I'll just have to take my lumps and leave the company gracefully." He returned to the safe and tried the door; it refused to budge. Grey of face he tottered to a chair and sat at the desk. "Thirty years of integrity down the drain." He rested his head on his hands and pressed fingers against his throbbing eyes.

"Is something the matter sir?"

Anstruther started to his feet, staring through the open doorway at the pyjama clad figure standing there. Small, about nine years of age with bold, enquiring eyes, the lad had about him that indefinable aura of confidence found in the children of the highly intelligent or sometimes the wealthy. "What? What's that?" he blurted.

"I asked if you needed help, Sir, is something wrong?"

One of Bradshaw's grandchildren was the thought which crossed Anstruther's mind. Now he was really in for it. He wanted to tell Bradshaw of his transgression first — now the kid would tell him.

The child was speaking again.

"Did I see you trying the safe, Sir? It's usually locked."

"Oh! Er! . . . No! . . . That is . . . Umm Yes."

The boy walked into the study, watching Anstruther, his eyes round and curious. "Why were you trying the safe?" He showed no fear, only interest.

George threw up his hands in defeat. "I was trying to get it open."

"Really? Are you a thief?"

George flushed beet red. "No I'm not a thief, I wanted to get something out. Something I put in and want to retrieve." His voice faltered and stopped. Who would believe a stupid story like that.

"What did you put in there, Sir?" The boy still sounded interested, not angry or frightened.

"I put a handkerchief in there." He saw a smug look cross the youthful face. "No really — I did it to get another man in trouble . . . and . . . Oh, why the hell am I telling you?"

"Why did you want to get him in trouble?" The boy's eyes, innocent, guileless, were fastened steadily on those of the embarrassed Anstruther.

"Because I was angry, stupid . . . And . . . And . . ." With many stops to gather his thoughts, George Anstruther poured out the accumulated sorrow and loneliness of his recent life, his need for work. "And so you see, I can't even hate my upstart successor enough to get him into hot water — I was trying to get the handkerchief back." He got to his feet and started heavily to the door.

"I can tell you how to open the safe, Mr. Anstruther."

George stopped and slowly turned. The boy was at the wall safe, idly flicking the dial left and right, left again. "Try ten left and seven right," he said.

George put his shaking hand on the dial and did as he was instructed, then gave the handle a twist. The door opened.

The child reached into the safe and pulled out the handkerchief. "Is this what you wanted?" He held the monogrammed linen out to Anstruther with one hand and swatted the safe door closed with the other.

George took the handkerchief. "Thank you," he stammered. "Thank you--but why?"

The child smiled impishly. "Perhaps it was the Christmas Spirit," he laughed. "Can't stay . . . I may be missed if I don't get back soon . . . Bye Mr. Anstruther, Merry Christmas," and he was gone.

"Merry Christmas sonny," stammered Anstruther.

It was late morning when he woke to a pounding on his door.

"Come on George, it's almost eleven."

"I'll be right there Thornby." Thornby again. He rushed his toilet and scrambled into his clothes, only then remembering the handkerchief. Had he put it in the safe? Had he really removed it — with the help of that child? Would the child tell Bradshaw? George set his jaw. I will not make a face; no matter how bitter the medicine, he thought, making for the stairs.

The grandfather's clock in the hall was striking the hour as he entered the large drawing room containing the Christmas tree.

"Well done, George," hailed Bradshaw from behind a red suit and white whiskers. "Thought you were going to disappoint us."

"Your beds are too comfortable — I nearly missed the festivities," returned Anstruther. "Would have if Thornby hadn't been good enough to give me a knock as he passed."

"We're glad you're here," said Mrs. Bradshaw — and sounded both sincere and pleased.

"Alright, here we go," shouted Bradshaw, diving a hand into

a pile of gifts. "First one is for . . . for Mavis Smithers. Come on Mave . . . give Santa a kiss."

"Enough of that Owen," laughed his wife. "You can have any girl you want for Christmas . . . as long as it's me."

Bradshaw joined in the laughter and slowly the pile of gifts diminished until there were only two left.

"The next to last gift is for Gilbert Thornby."

Funny, thought Anstruther, I never knew his name was Gilbert.

"Here Thornby, with our best wishes. And I wish to announce at this time that Gil Thornby is our new Vice President. Congratulations Gil." Bradshaw shook hands with Thornby and others called their good wishes. Some were looking at George with puzzled eyes. What was happening to Old George?

"And now I come to the most important announcement of the morning. Retirement is something we all try to forget, but that event comes along just when we least want it. It is all the more difficult when it is thrust upon us . . . sometimes before our time."

Why doesn't he get to the point and give me the boot? thought George. I can take it . . . now.

"So it is with me," continued Bradshaw. "Due to ill health I have been advised to step down as President and General Manager. In my place I have promoted the only man who has shown the selfless devotion needed for this position. Ladies and gentlemen, I give you George Anstruther." He grasped George's yielding hand and pumped it vigorously. "I'm putting you up for board membership at the next meeting," he whispered. "You'll get a seat for sure."

It was a dream fulfilled. George circulated, at first in a daze, then with confidence.

"I suppose I go back to calling you Mr. Anstruther now Sir," said Thornby with a tentative smile.

Anstruther gave him a long look — so long that Thornby started to wilt. "We'll be working pretty close, Gil. I'm told you have some sharp ideas we could use, we'll be together a lot. I think George will do fine for now."

Bradshaw appeared behind Anstruther while he was speaking. "Good man," he said. "I knew you had the ability, George, just a matter of putting you in the position." He glanced at Thornby. "Excuse us for a moment." He led Anstruther to the study. "Got a few things to sort out right away."

An hour later Mrs. Bradshaw called him for hors d'oeuvre.

"Before we go Mr. Bradshaw — where are the grand children?"

"Oh! There aren't any yet, old boy. Our son onl g t married last year — would have invited you, but it was around the time your wife passed away."

"But I saw a young boy last night . . . in the study. I came down to borrow a book and we talked." George Anstruther felt dizzy, and suddenly sat on the arm of a chair. No children! Who, or what had helped him at the safe last night.

"I say Anstruther, are you alright? There are no children in this house. None." Bradshaw gave a short laugh. "You must have been at the spirits, old boy. That's what it was. A little too much of the Christmas Spirit."

That was it . . . the drinks he had taken . . . pretty heavy ones. "I think you may be right, Sir. I might have taken a little too much."

George followed his host out of the study, and turned for a last look at the safe, closed tight in the far wall.

A small boy sat on the edge of the desk, still in pyjamas, his innocent face creased in a smile. He gave Anstruther a fat wink and put his finger to his lips.

George closed his eyes. When he opened them again the boy was gone.

"I guess that's what it was, Sir, Christmas Spirit," said George, catching up to Bradshaw. "The Spirit of Christmas." He made a mental note to return Gil's handkerchief, perhaps make it an excuse to have him drop by the flat. He'd like that — and he'd cut out scotch from now on.

Returning

CORALIE BRYANT

Christmas in Roseau (that prairie town)
many years ago
when we were kids
we remember
sometimes imperfectly
in detail
but perfectly
in emotion
surely
for how could a thing
so perfect, so powerful
live otherwise
in our hearts?
It was our mother's doing,
She
and the church;
no more than that
(except perhaps as Christ lived

through them
both).

The heavy carved wood panelling,
higharched stained windows
and long oak pews
made the church
cozy at Christmas
with white candles blazing
and the air heavy with the
incense of fresh cedar boughs
and Norway pine.
One tall tree freshly cut
and hauled from the woods
stood as high as the
cathedral ceiling,
presiding over solemn rituals,
the tallest Christmas tree
we had ever seen
(this was much before the town
began to erect its own
on the river bank
near where the
church then
stood).

A holiness
next to Christmas itself
was the Sunday
of the choir concerts;
Christmas really began then.
The big ones, including Dad,
sang with the senior choir,
the little ones in sweet and true

two and three-part harmony;
twice — at four o'clock and eight —
the candlelit church
filled to capacity
with faces from all over town
faces strange to our church
except at Christmas.
It was wondrous,
those new crinkly Christmas clothes
under white or green choir gowns;
the college kids — so much older
than a few months ago,
their voices strong, fuller
than their high school ones —
in the prized solos and quartettes,
guests of honor,
for they bestowed a dignity
to the occasion we could never
have managed alone.
But always Carl Dahlquist
sang *Jeg Jer Saa Glad*,
Don Norlin sent shivers down the spine
singing *O Holy Night*,
and whoever was the current
lucky loveliest mezzo soprano
made Christmas come
with *Lullaby on Christmas Eve*.

Mother didn't sing.
That is hard to believe now,
this woman in her seventies
who sings everywhere,
in trios and quartettes,
in costume and out,

sacred and silly stuff,
astonishing only
her children, never the people
who have lived by her
for fifty years. She stayed home
then: some of us
were too young to sing,
or there was too much to do,
or one of us was sick.
She sometimes came to hear us
in the evening, sometimes not.
One year we arrived home
to see a fireplace
against the wall
made ingeniously
from cardboard and red paper.
Stockings were hung.
We had never before had stockings.
Our hearts nearly stopped
for joy.

When I was older
my father would ask me
sometimes
on the morning of Christmas Eve
what I thought Mother would like
for Christmas.
The importance I felt
in being consulted
outweighed my outrage
on her behalf.
That he loved her
I knew.
That was enough.

I had learned
not to criticize
men or boys
much
but to please.
I remember picking out
plain brown wool
and a pattern —
the only thing I could think of —
and giving them to him to wrap somehow
so that she could make herself a dress.
I remember her eyes
when she opened the package.
Brown was not a good color for her,
wool bothered her skin,
this gift meant
more work,
it was not from
him to her
and she knew that.
(After he died
she found in his desk
a folder labelled
"Present Possibilities."
She was amazed to find
it filled with
ideas for presents —
written on
scraps of paper, or
circled in
clippings from
magazines and
catalogues — for her.)

But of all days of the year
in our home
this is the only one
I clearly remember
smell taste and hear
still. December 24th.
A day made not so much
by God
as by
our mother.

We had lists
in the morning, those
little white squares with
three or four chores written in,
a neat box before each
so we could check them off
as we finished.
The rules were never discussed,
only handed down
from child to child:
the lists stay on the table
so mother can check them
from time to time;
no one plays till the
work's done.
This applied also
on December 24th
until the whole house
shone.

We would all bundle up warmly
at four o'clock
to go caroling around the town

with the Junior Choir.
In cars or on foot, we'd go
from house to house
singing to invalids and
the old
in stale porches, or
sometimes invited
with our snowy boots
still on
into overheated living rooms,
sour-smelling and sad,
lit up by tree lights
and the beatific smiles
of the old gazing upon the young.

Poverty, illness and the lonely were
quickly forgotten as we stripped off
sodden scarves, mitts and boots, and
raced to change for Christmas supper.
The house smelled of lutefisk
and mashed potatoes and melted butter
and of flatbread and sweetpotatoes
and Swedish potato sausage (for the
only non-Norwegian at table,
Uncle Carl) and of pies and cookies,
of ginger, nutmeg, and brown sugar,
and of the tree, brought from the woods.
The table was already laid for nine,
and our cousins might already be
there, emptying boxes of gifts
carried in from the car
and putting them under the tree.
(When we were small,
Dad set the tree

into a playpen
to keep the younger kids
from tampering
with the gifts.)

Once a solemn grace was said,
we ate till we could not
stuff in one more bit of
lefse, spread and rolled
with butter and brown sugar
nor could we have stood
another minute of anticipation.
Time stood breathlessly
mercilessly
still
while the mothers
did the dishes,
the fathers talked
and smoked cigars
and we kids
prepared a program
to begin the evening —
another excuse, we thought,
to prolong our agony.

At last,
everyone sitting round,
we sang, and read Luke 2
and otherwise solemnly
summoned Christmas
as briefly as
we thought
we could get by with.
Finally, the moment:

the tension over which
child would be Santa
and deliver all the gifts,
the interminable
wait till it was our turn
to receive one,
tear it open,
wonder briefly about parents,
how *they* felt
opening their
presents
(could it possibly feel the same?)

When it was all over,
(how could that be? there
had been thousands of gifts!)
dessert and coffee and
platters of Christmas cookies and candy,
krumkaka, rosettes and sandbakkelse
would appear. How could
they interest anyone, we wondered,
as we reveled in our new things,
longing already for
Christmas morning,
when the real Santa
would bring something more,
something special —
once, even a phonograph
for the whole family.

Christmas Day brought Yulekaka,
(a merry Christmas breakfast bread),
church, and skating,
all afternoon,

hours to spend
at the rink
pushing our limbs to the limit,
then walking home in the biting
twilight air, exhausted, content,
and a little disappointed.
Only our parents, now
would disguise themselves in
silly costumes and
go Yulebakking
through the town,
singing and
fooling their friends, and then
plan New Years card parties
where we might have a sip of
Mother's homemade berry wine
if we were clever.
For us it was really all over,
December 25,
somewhere around five
in the afternoon.

Returning to the town where
we used to live —
the house and church
are gone
and so is Dad
but Mother is there
still making lefse
that melts in our mouths
and lutefisk that
makes us hunger
for our norske beginnings.
The house is hung with lights

and everywhere made gay for
her children's
and grandchildren's
glad homecoming.
And, going there, we now sing
altogether, round the tree,
as we did long ago with her,

The happy Christmas comes once more,
The heavenly guest is at the door.

The Bird Feeder

DONNA GAMACHE

"Wind's getting up," Sadie said to herself, as she watched the fresh snow begin to drift across the driveway. "I better feed my birds, before it gets worse."

She struggled into her old grey parka, the one she'd brought from the farm. "I just might need that old coat," she told Tom when they moved here last September. "Even in the city, there will be outside chores."

She measured out a cup of bird seed from the small bag from the supermarket and mixed it with bread crumbs. The bird seed was expensive, but on Christmas Day the chickadees should have a treat, though she knew they'd prefer sunflower seeds, as she used to feed them on the farm.

Pulling on an old pair of Tom's rubber boots and tying a faded red scarf over her grey hair, she hurried out the back door. "Look like the Friendly Giant in these boots, don't I?" she muttered. "I should throw them out."

But it was comforting, somehow, to see a pair of men's boots just inside when you opened the door. Even though there was no longer a man to use them. And nobody would see her, except for the small dark-haired boy next door. Sadie saw him now, as usual, with his nose pressed to the window, watching her every move.

As she expected, the bird feeder was almost empty. It was the one they'd used for years on the farm, a glass-fronted box into which you poured the feed. A narrow slit at the bottom let the seeds seep slowly out as the birds ate them.

The feeder was a dull grey now. Tom had painted it a deep green in the beginning, but the paint long ago washed off. It was one of the things Tom planned to fix, after they retired to this little house. But nobody had expected Tom's retirement days to be so short.

"Still works just as well," Sadie assured herself aloud. "Maybe next summer I'll get it painted."

She had nailed the bird feeder to the clothes line pole. It wasn't quite where she wanted it. But without Tom to put in another pole, she made do with the one already there. And at least she could watch the birds from her kitchen table.

"The feeder should be higher, too, shouldn't it?" she said to the single chickadee that perched in the nearby maple tree watching her. "It would be safer for you." But she'd put the feeder as high as she could reach from the ground. These days she wasn't steady enough to hammer while standing on a chair or box.

She'd done her best, even nailed a sheet of old tin around the pole to keep down cats. That big grey one next door, especially. She'd yelled at it several times since she began putting out the bird feed. She yelled at the boy, too, last week. "Keep your cat out of my yard! Away from my birds!"

Funny, she used to like cats, on the farm. But a cat in the city meant trouble for her birds.

She'd startled the boy; she knew that by the way he grabbed the grey cat and rushed inside. She'd regretted her harsh tone, but maybe it would teach him to keep his cat at home. A nice looking boy he was, though, about seven or eight, Sadie thought, with big dark eyes and dark hair. If she'd ever had a son, she'd have liked him to look like that. But she and Tom never had a son, just one tiny daughter, after many years of trying. And she was stillborn.

"There, that'll do you for today," she said now to the waiting chickadee. "I've given you extra bird seed. It's Christmas, you know. Even birds get treats."

She held out her hand to the chickadee, a few seeds on the palm. He watched, tilting his black cap a little to one side, but he was not to be tempted. "Well, I'll give you a few more days to get used to me," Sadie said. "Maybe you'll come yet. I always got at least one bird to eat from my hand, at the farm."

She turned to go, glancing at the house next door as she did so. A curtain moved, and the small boy ducked behind it. Black head and eyes--almost like a chickadee too, Sadie thought, then laughed at herself. "Wonder what kind of bird he thinks *I* am? Old grey parka. Faded red scarf. And giant feet." She snorted. "Red-headed woodpecker, I guess."

She stamped her feet at the back door, then pulled it shut behind her. "Red-headed woodpecker," she said again, hanging up the parka. "Wouldn't I love one of those at my feeder. Or a nuthatch. That would be nice, too." She *had* seen a downy woodpecker a few times. The corner store butcher had given her a piece of fat which she strung in the maple, and the little woodpecker came for that. But not often. Usually there were just one or two chickadees.

"Remember all the birds we had on the farm," she said, pouring herself a cup of coffee from the pot on the stove. "Woodpeckers, sparrows, half a dozen chickadees at least, a couple of blue jays, and evening grosbeaks by the dozen."

She sat at the kitchen table and peered out the window at the feeder. Her bird book lay on a nearby shelf, but she hadn't needed it since coming to the city. "Bring the book," Tom had said. "There are lots of parks in the city. We can take walks there. I'm sure you'll see birds. And in the winter we'll have a feeding station. Birds like the city, too."

But Tom had missed out on that. They'd moved the first week of September, and used the second week to settle into the tiny house, decide what to keep, and what, for lack of space, to throw out. But by the third week, Tom was gone, felled by a sudden stroke. And Sadie had to adjust not only to life in the city, but also to life alone. She took no walks in the park.

Sadie flicked on the radio and Christmas music filled the kitchen. It didn't feel much like Christmas; she'd never been alone before. Always there was Tom, and two or three neighboring families in for Christmas dinner, since she and Tom had no relatives nearby. But those neighbors lived fifty miles away now. The neighbors here, Sadie barely knew.

The Waynes across the street had left last week, for Florida or Mexico, or somewhere. And the Johnsons next door, Sadie had spoken to only briefly. Mr. Johnson was a salesman, often away; Mrs. Johnson worked nights and slept days; and the chickadee boy with dark eyes was usually at school, or alone in his yard.

Sadie felt tears threatening and blinked hard. She mustn't give in to self pity. "I can manage alone," she assured herself. "I'll watch the Christmas shows on television, and eat my chicken."

She'd tried to decorate the house a little. The wreath they used on the farm was now nailed on her front door, and Christmas cards hung on a string across one wall. But sympathy cards still occupied the china chest, an incongruous mixture, Sadie knew.

The doorbell rang, jarring through the gentle Christmas music. It rang so seldom here, it startled Sadie. "Whoever can that be?" She peered through the curtain before moving to open the door. "The chickadee boy! With a brown bag in his arms. What does *he* want?"

The bell rang again before she reached it. "I'm coming," she called. "Yes?" Her voice was sharp, she realized, and she smiled to soften the tone.

The boy hesitated. "I've — got a Christmas present for you," he managed. "Well, really it's for your birds." He held out the bag.

"Come in," Sadie said. "Don't stand there with the door open." The boy entered, lowering the heavy bag onto the floor.

"What is it?" she asked, unrolling the top. "Sunflower seeds!"

"We went to my uncle's farm yesterday," the boy blurted out. "I told him about your birds, the black and white ones. He gave me this from his granary. He grows sunflowers. Will your birds like these?"

Sadie smiled. "My birds will love them. The seed I get at the store isn't really what they want."

"What are they, your birds?"

"Chickadees. Black-capped chickadees. They're just like you, you know. Black cap and eyes. I call you the chickadee boy."

"My name is Todd," he said stiffly. "I'd better be getting home."

"Todd," Sadie nodded. "I thank you, Todd, for the present. My chickadees will love it." She closed the door, and watched him scurry down her driveway and back up his own.

"A present," she murmured. "*Real* birdfeed, this time." She carried the bag into the kitchen and set it on the counter, then glanced briefly outside. As she did, a grey and white streak ran head first down the maple tree, then flew quickly to the feeder and back to the tree. "A nuthatch! We hardly ever had those on the farm."

She watched him, marveling at his ability to walk head down. "A nuthatch," she said again. "A second Christmas present. I'm sure he'll like sunflower seeds, too."

Abruptly, the telephone shrilled. "Yes?" she answered.

The voice was hesitant. "This is Fran Johnson. Next door, you know? Todd says he thinks you're all alone there. Would you join us for Christmas dinner? We'll be eating about one."

"I don't want to intrude," Sadie ventured.

"It's no intrusion." The voice was firmer now. "We'd love to have you. I should have called you sooner. Just never thought of you being alone there. Please come."

"Thank you," Sadie said, feeling a new lightness in her voice. "I'll come. One o'clock."

She put down the phone and looked out the window where the chickadee and nuthatch seemed to be taking turns at the feeder. "But first," she said, "I have to feed my birds."

Starry Starry Night

DON BAILEY

This morning I boarded a plane in Winnipeg and flew twelve hundred miles to sit on a chair next to the person in the bed beside me. It was a last minute decision that upset the board and staff of the church where I am head honcho. They whined and wailed that the congregation would be upset by my absence. I didn't care. The truth is I don't care about anything. The last year of my life has been like living in a cave where the light is slowly diminishing, leaving me in the dark. I've come to offer comfort but also to seek the light.

I am not a person who acts on impulses, and the drama of using my influence as a clergyman to obtain a ticket for my son and me, claiming it was a life and death situation, the chaos of the airport, and the flight itself with many of the passengers drunk, expressing their emotional ambivalence towards the season by singing Christmas carols off key, has served to keep my mind off the purpose of the trip.

But now I am here. With my son. During the taxi ride from the terminal to my in-laws' Etobicoke home I was forced to face the fact that my actions are that of a man on the run. A man afraid to face certain truths about himself.

"This sure is a treat," the old man mutters. "You couldn't 've given us a better gift."

Joesph Edwin Bracknell, age 78, retired president of a discount shoe store chain he started himself from scratch. My father-in-law, grandfather to my son Mitchell, and father to my deceased wife, Bernice.

"People undervalue themselves," he says. "You get old and you realize the one thing you can't buy is time with the people you love."

He speaks with difficulty. The hospital bed he lies in is cranked up so he can watch the Christmas tree decorating going on in front of him. He has an IV going into each arm. One contains a solution to keep him from becoming dehydrated. The other feeds a steady flow of pain killer into his emaciated body.

Joe is dying. Three months after his daughter succumbed to cancer of the breast, his prostrate began acting up. It was removed but the surgeon said it was too late. Malignancy has set in and was deeply entrenched. Treatment would be useless.

No more fat Havana cigars or the daily half bottle of Crown Royale whiskey that functioned as a calming sedative to the explosive energy that drove him. He has lost sixty pounds from his six foot frame and food is of little interest to him.

"Sometimes when I'm lying here alone I feel like I'm in the middle of a movie," he says. "I mean it's like a dream where I'm sitting in the audience with my family. It must be a long time ago because the kids are all young, and we're holding hands, touching each other at least even if it's just our legs rubbing up against the next person, but I'm up on the screen too. In the picture, looking out at myself and everybody else. And I know how the story's going to end and I want to tell those who are watching that the ending's kind of sad, but it's worth their while to watch. The trouble is I can't say anything except what's in the script. There's no way I can change anything."

"I don't understand Joe," I say.

"Me neither Jake. It's probably just pharmaceuticals they're piping into me, making me see things."

"Joseph! his wife, Nancy, shouts from the step-ladder, "You're supposed to be resting."

She does not look our way but continues to hang the brightly colored glass balls on the huge scotch pine that reaches up to within six inches of the nine-foot ceiling.

"I'll get all the rest I need lying in the slumber room of Bardall's funeral home," he mutters. "After they run me through the walk-in barbecue they keep out back there won't be anything left of me but a pound and half of ashes that I want spread on the tomato plants in the Spring. Nothing like a little bone ash to pep up growing soil. Come August when those beefsteaks are as fat and juicy on the vine as I used to be, ripe for the picking, Nancy will be out there with her wicker basket gathering them up. And that night she'll have our sons over for dinner and I'll be reunited at the hearth of my family. In a manner of speaking. I just hope they remember my aversion to mayonnaise."

He chuckles by his mirth erupts in a bubbling, choking manner as though an aquarium has been implanted in his chest.

"None of that morbid talk Christmas eve," Nancy says. "We all know you're too stubborn to exit politely. Five years from now you'll still be laying in that bed pontificating on any subject that pops into your mind and I'll be up on this ladder, my joints as stiff as pig iron with this arthritis, probably slip, fall, break my neck, and be lying at your feet but you'll still be talking and won't even notice."

"You do your share pretty good too," he says.

"Have to," she replies. "A task assigned by God himself to remind you that there are others in the world beyond yourself.

A fact you've always found easy to forget."

"I resent being reduced to the cross you have to bear," he says. "You seem to be implying that I'm not the sensitive man I imagine myself to be."

Mitchell smiles. He is twelve years old and has a strong affection for the concept that life is a series of re-runs of his favorite television situation comedy. Since my own parents died many years ago I have no models of grandparents other than Joe and Nancy to offer him. I am afraid he will misconstrue their banter as a form of mutual love and respect.

"Don't concern yourself Joesph," Nancy says, as she stretches precariously on the ladder, balancing on one leg to place another garish decoration on the tree. "Forty-seven years and I have very few splinter scars to show for my efforts."

Mitchell laughs out loud. He is quick to pick up on their stinging humor.

The doorbell rings.

"That'll be the boys," Nancy says as she climbs down the ladder. She is a handsome woman. I would guess she is in her late sixties, her white hair cut short and permed into a fluffy cap that bounces as she strides across the living room towards the front hall.

"The anointed heirs," Joe says. "Glory be, they finally made it. Without us sending out a search party too. Good thing those two weren't part of the wise men trio. We'd still be waiting for them to find the Christ child. One of them would be in a drug rehab program and the other'd be taking an upgrading program in wisdom so he'd know what it was if it bit him on the ass."

Mitchell laughs loudly. He is sitting on the edge of the hospital bed with me next to him on a straight back chair, the theory being that Joe won't have to raise his voice to talk with us. My son takes his grandfather's hand in his own. He is the only grandchild. Neither of his uncles are married or even have girl friends they are serious about. Joe has made it clear that he views Mitchell as the only hope for the continuance of the family line. I worry that the boy will be spoiled by the attention that is lavished on him and the money he's liable to inherit.

Nancy stops in the hall and directs a fierce look at Joe. She opens one of the French doors and shouts at him.

"You behave," she says. "Your sons may not have turned out like you but that might be its own kind of blessing."

"Well disguised if you ask me," he says.

"At least when the time comes for them to retire their wives won't have to put up with the chairman of the board calling in the middle of the night begging for help to ease them out."

"Biggest mistake I made," Joe says. "Letting the company go public. Don't know who was greedier, me or the stock holders. But for different things. I wanted their capital to expand but they just wanted to park their dough in a safe cove so they could collect dividends into the twenty-first century. Spent all my time fighting with them."

"And always got your way," Nancy says.

The doorbell rings but she doesn't move.

"No danger of those two ever having trouble with the board," he says. "I suppose with the voting block we still hold you could demand seats for them on the board. I still own over forty per cent of the company but the lawyers, bankers, and accountants would fight it. The thing is neither one of them knows the difference between cow slips and slippers. As far as wives are concerned, I don't think either one's got the energy to engage in the battle of the sexes."

"They're just slow starters," she says. "As long as I represent this family on the board, they'll have a place if they so choose."

The doorbell rings again and Joe releases a soft chuckle.

"Haven't even got the sense to try the door. Is it locked?"

"No," she says, moving to open it. "They were brought up to be polite. More than I can say for some others who are cluttering up the environment with their moaning about dying."

"I'm a sick man, Nancy, and I've got the puncture marks to prove it."

"Well no dying tonight," she says. "You do and I'll be tempted to drag you out to the curb beside our blue box so you can be recycled with the tin cans."

Mitchell bounces on the bed in appreciation, laughing so hard the sound becomes locked in his throat. Nancy opens the door and her two sons enter. At the same moment the live-in registered nurse appears from the dining room, a glass of amber liquid in her right hand. She walks over to Joe's bed and checks the IVs. She pops a thermometer into the old man's mouth and takes his pulse as she waits for his temperature to register.

"Enjoying my rye Elsie?" Joe asks, as she completes her check of his vital signs.

"Smooth as an infant's behind," she says, taking a large gulp from the crystal glass that she then holds up to the light and admires.

"How 'bout pouring me one," he asks.

She releases a guttural chuckle and points to the two men entering the room.

"Your boys are here," she says. "You best be keeping your wits about you."

"Later then," he says, negotiating hard.

She tugs at the white material of her uniform that is as thick as tent canvas and hangs from her wide, middle-aged body like a protective tarpaulin.

"Perhaps when the tree's finished," she says. "A small one when the angel's put in place. To celebrate the season."

"We top our tree with a star," Nancy says.

"Whatever symbol suits you best," Elsie says with a shrug and saunters off towards the dining room where she will sit at the table in the dark, watching and listening as she nurses a glass of seasonal spirits.

Paul, the oldest of Joe's sons, enters the room briskly. He leans over the bed and plants a loud, wet kiss on his father's forehead.

"Geezus," the old man protests, "wait 'til I stop breathing before you start slobbering over me."

The younger son, Larry, who will be thirty-five his next birthday, squeezes out a laugh that is similar in sound to the steel wheels of a locomotive screeching to a halt.

Paul smiles painfully. Blonde, pale like his mother, he steps back from the bed and clasps his hands together in front of him, his thirty-eight-year-old face unlined by worldly concerns. A man committed to fierce politeness.

"I'm pleased to see you in such fine spirits, father," Paul says.

In his dark blue, three piece suit he looks like an accountant and has the carefully controlled speech of a funeral director. I have tried during my fifteen years of being part of this family to warm to Paul, to connect with him, but some inadequacy within me has sabotaged this possibility. Although his name is biblical in its origins and therefore has some historical substance, the Paul holding his hand out to me is elusive, unrevealing. He makes me feel like a visitor from another planet.

"Good to see you Jake," he says. "Surprised but pleased."

His hand slides out of mine and stops in front of Mitchell who stands and grapples with it awkwardly.

"Hi Uncle Paul," the boy says.

"You've grown Mitchell."

"Yes," the boys answers.

"That's what kids do," Joe says. "You haven't seen him in almost a year. Don't be such a tight-ass, give the kid a hug."

Paul ignores his father's remark, removes his suit jacket, folds it carefully, and places it on the back of an upholstered chair. He turns towards me and we have eye contact for a second or two. His eyes make me think of two pools of murky brown mud that serve as cloudy windows so that it is impossible to know the inner rage I suspect he harbors. Both he and his brother exist on weekly allowances provided by their mother. She sends a monthly cheque to their landlords so they are assured of a place to live. Since neither brother has a car, she shops weekly for their groceries and delivers them to their apartments. When they need clothes, mother takes them on an excursion where she foots the bill and, for the most part, decides what they'll wear. I always wondered how their sister Bernice had turned out so differently. A rebel who depended on no one.

"I would have thought a clergyman would be in great demand to his congregation at this time of year," Paul says.

"I work in a team ministry," I reply. "Everyone else's taken holidays this year so I decided it was my turn."

"That's reassuring," he says. "When mother informed us you were coming I thought father's death was imminent. We only ever seem to see you at family funerals."

"Cute," Joe says. "Very cute Paul, but mean . . . No call for it . . . The medical profession has turned my body into an irrigation system and I've been ready to dry up and blow away for months now . . . They seem to believe that as long as I'm wet, I'll keep living. I feel like a patch of desert that the Israelis are trying to revitalize, pumping stuff into me at one end and collecting it at the other end. Speaking of which . . . Elsie! You gonna empty this bladder bag or let it run all over the carpet?"

"I checked it not ten minutes ago," she calls from the other room. "It's not even half full."

Larry, tall and thin in baggy jeans and a flannel shirt that hangs outside his pants, comes over to the bed and pokes at the plastic container being discussed.

"She's right Pop," he says. "Still plenty of room in the old piss bag.'

Curious, Mitchell leans down to have a look. Nancy bustles over to the ladder next to the tree and scurries up to the last rung.

"Com'on boys," she says. "Your father's been waiting all night for you to come and finish the decorations."

"I'm taking a shower first," Larry announces. "Downstairs."

"Good idea," Joe says. "While you're down there have a look around for the garden shears. You find them, bring them up and I'll shorten that mop of hair by a foot or two."

The younger son laughs and pats his father gently on the shoulder.

"You haven't been paying attention," he says. "The sixties are back. Long hair is in again."

"You look ridiculous," his father says.

"Maybe," Larry says, "but then I guess so did Jesus. He was the first hippy. Right Jake?"

"And look what they did to him," I answer as a means of deflecting the question.

The old man releases a bubble of laughter.

"They nailed him good," he says. "Is that what you want Larry? A bunch of people come along and hammer you on to a cross?"

The smile on Larry's face collapses into an expression of dismay. I think he imagines that these kind of exchanges with his father are all in good fun but Joe isn't joking. The old man festers with rage and resentment over the failure of his sons to follow the trail he has laid out for them.

But Larry is resilient. The smile returns to his face and he looks at his father with affection.

"You're right Pop," he says. "A person should have a reason for being wierd. For me it's just a habit. Speaking of which, how is the church business these days Jake?"

Paul has joined his mother at the tree. She is hanging tinsel on the upper branches while he works on the bottom half.

"Finished for me," I say. " I put in my resignation for April."

"You're transferring to a new congregation?" Joe asks.

"I hope its closer to Toronto," Nancy says. "That one time we visited you in Winnipeg was unbearable. So much cold can't be good for your health. My tulips were blooming the day we left here and but when we stepped off the plane, a blizzard was blowing."

"I'm leaving the ministry."

Nancy cannot hide her surprise. She squats down and sits on the top step of the ladder.

"What're you going to do Jake?" she asks.

"My Dad's gonna get a nine-to-five job," Mitchell says. "Like all my friends' parents have. You know like a real job."

Everyone laughs but I sense an undercurrent of uneasiness.

"I haven't decided," I say. "All I know is that I want to do something different, something where I can see some tangible results that I think are worthwhile."

"What could be more satisfying than overseeing the spiritual live of your flock?" Nancy asks. "I can understand wanting to change the location, God knows we'd be happier having you and Mitchell closer at hand . . . but to give up the whole thing . . . "

"I'm not a happy shepherd," I answer. "And anyway, the sheep are restless. Couples used to come to me for marriage counselling, now they're urging me to use the church to set up some kind of tax shelter so they can avoid income tax. They want my blessing on their decision to put their parents in nursing homes so they can get power-of-attorney and take control of the old folk's money before they spend it on foolishness like touring the country on a motorcycle. The visiting committee has me video-taping my sermons so shut-ins don't have to be picked up and lugged to the church Sunday mornings. We have a campaign to raise money to buy VCRs for any senior in the congregation who doesn't have one. Pretty soon I'll be able to FAX the service to everyone's home and no one will have to come to church."

"Sounds like you've let them shake your faith," Nancy says.

"Too heavy for me," Larry says as he clomps off towards the basement.

"Let's listen to what Jake has to say," Joe says.

"Perhaps, he's thinking of going into shoes," Paul says. "He might persuade our board to set up a charitable foundation to shoe the barefoot of the world. Reeboks for Russian waifs, Converse for cannibals. We could unload our mismatched sizes on third world countries and the government would probably allow us a huge write-off. We could call it the Ministry of Soles."

I laugh.

"Not a bad idea," I say, "Sounds like a more honest hustle that what I'm doing now."

"Don't turn cynic on us Jake," Nancy says. "We've got enough of those around here to do us."

"What's that mean Dad?" Mitchell asks.

"A cynic is a person who goes around bursting people's balloons because he hasn't got one himself," Joe says.

"My Dad's not like that," the boy says.

"No, he's not," the old man says, "but your grandmother is worried about what he'll do when his job is finished in Winnipeg. Me too."

"I'll be fine," I say. "University of Toronto have offered me a teaching position in their theological department. Three courses a semester. Less work and more money."

"So you won't really be leaving the church," Nancy says. "Just doing something different. Well a change is good, healthy even. When will you start?"

"Next Fall but I haven't accepted it," I reply. "I'm still thinking about it. The other idea I had was to write a book about ministries in the inner city. All the churches I've worked for have been in the heart of the city and what I learned is that they're all dead. Some of them preserved beautifully, and visited weekly by all the faithful who live ten, fifteen miles away in the suburbs. But what about the people who live a block from the church, the students, the single mothers and their kids, the old people in small rooms cooking their margarine casseroles on hot plates? How come they don't attend and fill some of the space in the empty pews?"

"You can't expect people like that to keep a church going. They don't have the money and they have too many other problems to cope with. They're too busy surviving to have an appreciation for a good sermon. You should know that!" Nancy says. "If people drive in from the suburbs, ten, fifteen miles every week it just shows how committed they are. You should be happy they continue to be loyal."

"You're probably right," I say, "but twenty years ago when I was ordained I had this idea that our ministry was supposed to respond to the needy, heal the wounded, feed the masses . . . no one said anything about comforting the complacent."

"Well you're a fool if you think people are going to pay out money for a book that tells them their church is a corpse. People want good news, not bad. There's enough bad news going around for free."

She stands up on the ladder again and resumes hanging tinsel on the tree. Elsie sidles into the room with a triumphant grin on her face.

"He's doing it again," she says.

"What're you talking about?" Joe asks.

"Wacky tobacky," she says. "Number two son is toking up in the basement and blowing the smoke into the heating ducts."

"I can't smell anything," Nancy says.

Mitchell runs over to a heating vent on the floor, sprawls down, and puts his face against it. He breaths in deeply.

"Yup," he announces. "That's grass."

"How would you know?" I ask.

"Quite a few guys at my school smoke pot," he says. "Especially before math or science classes."

"You thought about private school for this boy?" Joe asks. "I'll be glad to pay the freight."

"That wouldn't do any good Grandpa," Mitchell says. "My hockey team plays against a private school and half their players get stoned before they go on the ice. They says it makes them calmer, helps them concentrate so they score more goals."

"Crap!" the old man bellows. "That stuff will rot your brain. You stay away from it Mitchell."

"I will," the boy says.

"Paul, go downstairs and speak to your brother. He knows I won't stand for that stuff in my house. If he has to use it, tell him to stick his head in the vent for the dryer. That way at least the smoke'll blow outside."

Paul puts his suit jacket back on and heads towards the basement. Nancy comes down the ladder and steps back to look at the tree. She then plugs in the Christmas lights and the tree gives off a shimmering multicolored glow.

"I think it's the best one we've ever had," she says.

"A beauty," Joe says. "But what about the star?"

"I'm going to make some egg nog first," she says. "Then we'll put it up."

"Can I help?" Mitchell asks.

"Of course," she says, and the two of them troop off to the kitchen.

"I might as well pitch in," Elsie says from the dark dining room.

"What about my drink?" Joe asks.

"In due time," Elsie replies as she too heads towards the kitchen.

Paul and Larry enter the living room through the French doors.

"We've gotta go," Paul says. "Larry's not feeling well. I've got a friend's car so I'll drive home."

"What's the matter?" Joe asks.

Larry takes his coat from the hallway closet and turns towards his father. "I just don't seem to be in the Christmas spirit," he says.

"Your mother'll be upset," Joe says. "We hardly ever see you."

"She sees lots of me," Larry says. "It's you and I that avoid each other. Saves us a lot of grief."

"Well speak to her before you leave."

"I'd rather not," he says. "She'll just try to talk me into staying."

He puts on his coat and heads towards the front door.

"You'll be coming back Paul?" Joe asks.

"I'll try," his son answers.

They open the door quietly and slip out into the cold winter night.

Joe and I sit quietly for a few moments. I feel embarrassed for the old man. He is too tired to express the anger I imagine he must feel. Suddenly he grabs my hand and squeezes it tightly. We can hear laughter coming from the kitchen.

"What's that Psalm about the shepherd Jake?" he asks.

"The Lord is my shepherd, I shall not want. He makes me lie down in green pastures; He leads me beside quiet waters. He restores my soul; He guides me in the path of righteousness for His name's sake . . . Even though I walk through the valley of death, I fear no evil; for thou art with me. . ."

"Yeah," he says. "That's the one. I've never been a religious person but one of the last times I saw Bernice . . . You were living out at the river house and she and I sat out on the lawn watching the stars come out . . . . She was only a week from dying and I didn't have a clue what to say . . . I never felt so helpless. There was nothing I could do to fix the situation but she took my hand and recited that psalm . . . I think it was more to comfort me that her . . . And then she pointed up to the sky, at the stars . . . She told me that stars were planets that had died but thousands of year later they were still burning . . . even the sun is a star . . . without them we'd be living in darkness. Before I got sick I'd always go walking at night and look up and the first star I saw always made me think of her . . . How do you remember her Jake?"

"I try not to Joe," I reply.

"Yeah, that's what I thought. Mitchell's the same. The two of you never mention her . . . It's not good for you Jake. Memories are like matches we strike to light up the gloom. I remember we stayed at this cottage one year and Bernice dragged me out of bed in the middle of the night to come outside with her to watch the fire-flies. I thought she'd prob- ably want to catch them and put them in jars. That's the kind of thing I did when I was a kid. But not her. She just wanted me to sit with her on the porch and watch these bugs flickering in the dark. She called them flying stars."

"I miss her terribly," I admit.

"I know you do," he says. "And the world's full of things that will remind you of her. Don't cut off your head and heart to your history, Jake. From what I saw, you and Bernice had your share of happiness. The future's just a black hole if you don't use those memories to blaze a new trail for you and Mitchell."

"Do I seem so unhappy?" I ask.

"You cover it up well," he says. "But quitting the church I think is your way of withdrawing from the limelight. You can hide out pretty good in a university. Get lost in the shuffle. Writing a book is even a better way of disappearing inside yourself."

"You're a pretty smart guy, Joe."

He smiles and grips my hand harder.

"Come work for me," he says. "We've got a store downtown that needs a manager. People need shoes as much as they need salvation."

"I'll think about it," I say with a smile.

"At least with shoes," he says, "you know whether the customer is satisfied or not before they leave the store. There's a certain gratification in that Jake."

"I can see that," I say.

"So you'll do it?" he asks eagerly.

"Maybe when we come in April, I'll try it. For a few months anyway."

"Good," he says. "You won't regret it Jake. A couple of months in the store and we can move you up. A year or two and you could be running the operation. Take a load off Nancy."

Suddenly I feel alarmed. This is not why I came. I have no desire to run a foot-wear empire. Being this close to Bernice's family will be too painful. For both Mitchell and me.

"Listen Joe, this would just be a temporary thing. I can't imagine myself filling your shoes, which it sounds to me like you want me to do."

He laughs softly.

"Filling my shoes . . . yes I guess that's it."

"I couldn't," I say. "Paul and Larry should be the ones."

"I'll leave that up to you," he says, his voice growing fainter. "Right now I've got to have a nap."

His eyes close and his breathing becomes shallow. In a minute or two his hand grows limp in mine. I am still holding it when Nancy, Mitchell, and Elsie enter the room. My son is carrying the punch bowl of egg nog which he sets on a table. Elsie has two glasses of whiskey.

"Time for the star to go up," Nancy announces, and then she looks around the room. "Where are the boys?"

"Larry was feeling sick," I say. "Paul drove him home."

"Oh." says Nancy. "It's always been a tradition for one of the children to place the star. Bernice did it when she was small. And then the boys."

"I'll do it," Mitchell volunteers.

Nancy hands him the star while Elsie puts down the two glasses of whiskey on the bedside table and checks Joe's vital signs. She says nothing but removes the old man's hand from mine and places it gently across his stomach. She picks up her own glass and hands the other one to me.

Mitchell is at the top of the ladder where he places the large silver star carefully on the peak of the tree.

"That's beautiful!" Nancy exclaims. "Look Joe, isn't the star lovely."

"He's asleep," I say.

She glances over at him and smiles. The she heads to the punch bowl and ladles out a cup of egg nog which she raises in the direction of the tree.

"It's never truly Christmas for me," she says, "until the star's in place."

Mitchell fills a cup and we all join in a silent toast.

A Christmas Story

ROY BONISTEEL

Usually when you live on a mixed farm you can count on a few dollars from at least one source, even if other crops or pursuits fail. But the fall of 1944 found our family approaching Christmas with no cash. We had enough to eat and we could certainly count on a plump turkey or chicken for the festive dinner, and of course we had our own Christmas tree. It was just that there was no money for the extras. Despite this, my father told my mother to go ahead and buy what she needed, since the friendly merchants in Trenton would give us credit until after the holidays. Our ace-in-the-hole was the woodlot. As soon as we got a few inches of snow we would go into the woods and cut enough firewood to pay off our debts.

A week before Christmas the snow started. Big fat flakes that just kept piling up until the fence tops disappeared. Two days before Christmas the snow plow came down our dead-end road and turned around in the barn yard. It was a large wooden V loaded with boulders and pulled by a four-horse team. The driver gave the horses a rest while he stomped the snow off his boots and came into the kitchen for a cup of hot coffee.

"They've got it a lot worse back around Stirling," he said. "Some drifts over eight feet high. By the way, are you selling any wood this year? Sam Barton told me to ask if I saw you. He's right out and looks like he might have a pretty cold Christmas." Sam Barton lived on the ninth concession with his wife and four children. He worked the old Homer place on shares and often bought a few cords of wood from us, usually later on in the New Year.

On the afternoon before Christmas, my older brother Bert and I piled two stacks of dry, split wood, each eight feet by four feet by four feet, on to the stake body of the old Fargo truck and started out through the still falling snow on the ten mile trip to the Barton place. The truck's heater never worked well, but we were bundled up warmly and the cab was small enough that body heat was sufficient. Bert played a mean harmonica, and while my singing voice left a lot to be desired, I knew all the words to most songs. As we made our way slowly through the thickening snow we tortured every tune on the current hit parade and assaulted every Christmas carol that came to mind.

It was almost five and we had turned on the Fargo's one good headlight by the time we spotted the Barton mailbox and drove up the snow-filled ruts of the lane. Sam and his wife and the four noisy youngsters made us feel like the relief of Dunkirk as they greeted us warmly and began to unload our precious cargo. When we had finished, Sam asked Bert how much he owed.

"Same as last year. Dad said not to charge any more just because it's dry. That's twelve dollars a cord and a dollar for gas."

I was thinking that twenty-five dollars would certainly help Mom pay off what she owed for Christmas presents when I heard Sam say, "To tell the truth, I'm a little short this year. All I can spare is twenty dollars."

Bert hesitated. Mrs. Barton looked embarrassed and hopeful

at the same time. She said, "Let me give you a nice capon. It's already dressed and ready for the oven. My chickens were the only thing we had any luck with this year!"

"That'll be just fine, ma'am," said Bert.

I waited until we were out of the driveway and turned towards home before I said, "Dad's going to be some mad that you're short five dollars. And the last thing in the world we need is a chicken."

"What was I supposed to do?" asked Bert. "Put the wood back on the truck?"

The snow was still falling in earnest and a cold east wind had started piling drifts diagonally across the road. The truck, now without its weighty ballast, was skidding dangerously as the wheels carved new tracks behind the pale glow of our single headlight. The windshield and windows were becoming thick with frost and we took turns scraping clear a small peep-hole on the driver's side.

It was at the corner of the fifth concession, still about five miles from home, that we went off the road. The back wheels swerved over the edge of a hidden culvert and we slid silently and deeply into the snow-filled ditch.

"The Creighton place is a little over a mile west," said Bert. "He'll have a tractor to pull us out."

We had trudged only about a hundred yards through the storm, and I was thinking what a cold, miserable Christmas eve it had turned into, when we saw a light coming from the window of a small house off to the side of the road.

"Who lives there?" I shouted over the wind.

"I don't know." Bert stopped and peered through the trees that lined the front yard. "I think it used to be an old tenant house, but somebody has fixed it up. Let's give it a try."

We were just about to knock on the door when Bert said, "Look!" Through the curtainless window I saw the strangest sight I had seen in my fourteen years. An old man, bald except for a grey fringe over his ears and wearing faded red long johns, was dancing spryly around the room — with a dog. A handsome, well-groomed collie had both front paws planted firmly on the man's shoulders and was awkwardly but purposefully striding back and forth. We could hear the music and could see a wind-up phonograph in the corner of the room.

Bert and I looked at each other, then back down the road, where the truck was fast becoming invisible, and finally knocked on the door. We heard the music stop and slippered feet shuffle to the door. It was opened wide and we felt the warmth of a roaring wood fire hit us as the man beckoned us quickly inside.

Bert said, "Our truck has slid into the ditch at the corner. I was wondering if you had a tractor I could borrow to pull it out."

"Sure have, young feller. Got a small Allis-Chalmers in the shed behind the house should do the trick. Take off those coats and sit for a minute first. You must be frozen. Don't worry about your boots."

As he motioned us to a slip-covered hobo couch to one side of the fireplace, I took off my coat and glanced around the room. It was small but neat. In the centre was a kitchen table and two curved-back chairs. A rocking chair was pulled up near the fire. A large kitchen cupboard dominated the far wall, and the other three were hung with framed calendar prints of mountain ranges, seascapes, and floral arrangements.

"How about a hot drink?" he asked. Without waiting for an answer, he took an earthen jug and some glass tumblers from the cupboard and put them on the table. Grabbing the poker from the hook over the fireplace, he pushed it deep into the red coals below the burning logs. He turned and smiled at us.

"Wasn't expecting company. Not many people stop in here. My own fault, I guess. Rose and I never made many friends out here. Oh well, it's too late now." He stood with one hand on the poker and stared at a small photograph over the mantel. It showed a laughing woman with thick long hair, head thrown back, eyes bright and full of humor.

"We moved here over three years ago from the Maritimes when I retired from the shipyard. Always wanted to get a small farm. Rose had a real green thumb. Grew vegetables. Didn't make much, but we were sure happy!"

The end of the poker was glowing red now. He removed it slowly and plunged it into the jug on the table. A hiss of steam erupted and filled the room with the smell of apple cider. He poured us each a glass full and took his to the rocking chair. The first swallow of the warm liquid seemed to bounce off my empty stomach and brought tears to my eyes. I felt little tingles in my brain and realized that it certainly wasn't this year's crop. I glanced sideways at Bert and saw him smiling appreciatively. He was not the stranger I was to hard cider. The old man finished his drink in one long, thirsty gulp and absently poured himself another. He poked the fire needlessly.

"She died. Died two years ago. Just like that." He snapped his fingers but no sound came. "Not a day goes by but I miss her. Like an ache it is. Sure miss her at Christmas. It was a special time for us. Didn't pay much attention to the religion part of it, but the love part was sure there. Maybe it's the same, I don't know. We'd make presents for each other, decorate the place with some crepe paper and always had a roast goose or chicken. I can make a real good stuffing.

"I got good memories. Some minister came by after and said not to worry because Rose wasn't dead, she was living on in heaven. I guess he meant well. I know Rose is dead and the only place she lives on is in my memories. Maybe that's what heaven is — memories."

A log fell in the fire and sent a shower of sparks up the chimney. This seemed to rouse him from his reveries and he noticed that both his glass and Bert's were empty. I was still taking small sips from mine and thinking the warm room was making me woozy. "There's plenty more," he said.

"Thanks, but I'd better get the truck out," answered Bert. Then, with a glance at the old man, he said to me, "You stay here and keep warm. I can yank it out by myself."

"Be careful of the crank, it kicks sometimes," he said as Bert buttoned his coat and went out the door. With his glass refilled, he sat down by the fire and in a minute continued talking. His dog yawned and stretched closer to the fire.

"She was an English girl. Met her on Christmas eve at a dance in Liverpool during the last war. I couldn't dance worth a hoot but she showed me how. Would you mind putting that music back on?"

I went over to the phonograph and gave the handle a couple of turns then dropped the arm over the edge of the record. The music started as I returned to the couch.

"That piece is called *Greensleeves*. It's an English tune. We danced to it that first night. It's a waltz, you know. Rose taught me how to make a box pattern with my feet. One-two-three . . . one-two-three. We laughed so much. We got married while I was still in the navy, then after the war we came to Canada. Got off the boat in Halifax and decided to stay there. Lots of good years. Never had kids. Didn't seem to matter. Had each other."

The music stopped and the needle made a scraping sound in the last groove. He started to sing in a low, halting voice:

Alas, my love! ye do me wrong
To cast me off discourteously:
And I have loved you so long,
Delighting in your company.

I went over to the machine, lifted the arm and turned off the turntable.

"I heard they made a Christmas carol out of that piece," he said. "Makes sense. It's always been a Christmas song to me."

He was humming now and staring into the fire. I heard the tractor come up beside the house and sputter to a stop in the shed. Bert came through the door in a blast of cold air. The old man didn't even look up. I put on my coat.

"Thank you very much," my brother said. "We really appreciate your help." There was no reply from the figure by the fire that rocked and hummed. Bert took from under his mackinaw the fat capon and set it on the table beside the cider crock. "Goodbye," we both said as we backed out the door. The dog thumped his tail twice on the floor in acknowledgement.

The snow was tapering off and by the time we got to the second concession it had stopped completely. Neither of us spoke on this final leg of our journey. As we started down our own dead-end road, the moon broke through and shot blue shadows over the snow drifts. I could see the lights ablaze from every window of our farm house as we drew near and I thought of Christmas Day, just a couple of hours away. With the snowfall ended, my other brothers and sister and my aunts and uncles would be able to come. There would be laughter and games and shouts of joy as we opened our almost-paid-for presents. Loved ones, together.

As we turned up the lane towards the yellow lamplight spilling over the snow, Bert had his harmonica out again. He was softly playing *What Child Is This?*

On Christmas Eve: 1963

JOAN FINNIGAN

Dear Country Cousin:

Tonight, the night before Christmas, it is inevitable that my thoughts should turn to you. I think of you there on that wilderness farm with the road across the fields growing narrower, narrower in the vise of winter and not even the light of a neighbor to be seen in the distance, and I feel momentarily that I would gladly trade your clean stretch of stars for the gaudy insistent neons of my road here.

I think of how it will be in your house, shadowy with lamplight and warm with the heat of the stove, the cats curled up in the wood-box and the dogs on the mat by the door. You will be trying to get the last of your brood into their beds upstairs, and one, probably Jackie, the eldest, dreamer and watcher of wild birds, will be pressing his nose for the last time against the frosted pane, straining for a look at the sky, sensing it different tonight, full of expectations and mysteries.

It's many a year and event undreamed of that's gone by since you and I were his size, swallowed up in the great warm cocoon of our grandfather's house, pressing our noses against the bay windows of the big dining-room, watching sleighs swing through the gate and into the yard. And what excitement as the buffalo robes disgorged the drivers and passengers, some uncles, some aunts, some cousins, perhaps our great blue-eyed giant of a grandfather returning from a Trip to Town!

They would cross the veranda and lift the latch on the kitchen door and enter like great fat furry bears and stomp their feet of snow. Such a stomping in those heavy boots! We stood, terribly small and wide-eyed, wondering if such stomping would not take them through the floor right into China. Looking back now I don't think it was necessary to shake the dishes in the cupboard like that at all, but I think it was a way of a man announcing his arrival back into the household. And then, too, in that country, Pontiac County, to be a good stomper was the earmark of a good dancer.

The horses, the carriage-shed, the house, the buffalo robes, even some of the people, are gone now, but in my mind the sleds have sprouted wings, still fly, glistening, graceful as swans, jingling through the wintry roads of my childhood journeys. Time has graciously embellished them with even greater magic than they had for me then. And I can't think of the sleigh-rides I had through the white castles of the snow in the dark nights of the country without also thinking of the train up the Pontiac from Ottawa — the Push-Pull-and-Jerk I think they called it when they wrote its obituary several years ago and took it off the lines.

Many was the time this nose was pressed to the pane of that slow train winding along the Ottawa River into the dusk of the winter's evening. Many were my grave fears of missing the station, of the conductor going to sleep somewhere back on the mailbags and letting me miss my station and of my ending up in Mattawa with no grandfather or uncle walking the station platform to keep himself warm in the wait, no little black horse named May stomping her feet and tossing her head by the rail. But always he came, faithfully down the aisle, to a child lost behind the dusk and the glazed windows and sounded out my salvation by calling, "Shawville, next stop." I had had my bag clutched in my hand since Luskville, my hat and coat on since Quyon and there never was a racer at the starting-post so poised as I for the descent, the incredibly exciting descent down those train steps — I can see them yet, corrugated steel encrusted with ice — into the welcome of the waiting relative.

Then we would wrap ourselves up in the sleigh and take to the air and fly the snow-ways like a black bird, the clip-clop of the little horse beating out the rhythm of our wings. And we would beat our heavenly passage through the dark to the light of my grandmother's lamps, to the warm kitchen of her perennially ready suppers, to the great downy ticks of the high beds in the cold rooms and the house cracking and groaning as I fell like Alice in Wonderland down the long, long passage of sleep.

Somehow I can't think of all those mysterious things without remembering Joker.

Did you know, country cousin, that whenever the men came back from the lumber camps to the farm at Radford, that old collie would drop out of the winter's night onto their sleigh when they were yet many miles from home and had sent no word, indeed, could not send any word of their impending arrival? By some dog-mystique he knew that they had started out from the Rouge River, and he would begin his "incredible journey" and descend upon them like a wraith out of the night as they hurried through the last lap of their journey, still many miles from home. He did that for ten years, and he, too, has become in my mind a sort of inexplicable dog-spirit of uncanny devotion still abroad in our valley.

Remember all the days, too, we spent tugging toboggans to the hills or trekking along wintry roads to the houses of other cousins who always took us in, fed us and wrapped us up for the night. When you arrived by foot it was always implicitly, and, to me, mysteriously understood that you were "staying the night." There was no invitation issued; preparations were simply made for such an event, which was welcomed by the inhabitants of the farmhouse in the lonely days and nights of their cut-off winters.

And I cringe yet in memory of the "Time of the Wolf Tracks." Do you remember one day when we had gone to the farthest extremities of the farm in search of the highest hill? And there, out of sight of habitation and in the furious house of the wind I espied in the snow before our very eyes — wolf tracks! Nothing you could say could dissuade me from that conviction: not that they were Joker's tracks in the snow as he chased his old enemy, the ground-hog; not that it was the neighbor Hanna's dog; nothing. They were wolf tracks, and without even so much as one slide down that long-sought hill, I forced you to turn back and head for the safety of the big house, to the spirit of warmth and light it exuded without central heating or electric lights.

Yes, spirit. That is what I am looking for as I write to you tonight, as my mind turns to your farm at the foot of the Brule Hill.

I know a very wise grandfather here who was asked by his grandchildren, "What is spirit?" And he answered this way: He held up his hand and blew his breath between his fingers upon their upturned faces.

"Can you see that?" he asked.

"No," came the reply.

"Can you feel it?"

"Yes," came the chorus.

"That is spirit, my children," he said.

Ah spirit! That is the thing I am seeking here in the city upon this Christmas eve, and somehow I always have such a difficult time finding it here that I turn to thoughts of you, my country cousin, and, in the vicarious contemplation of the peace and beauty and tranquility in which you live, I seem to find what I am looking for.

I think perhaps other people find their minds turning like this upon a Christmas eve, from the crowded turbulence of the city to the primitive peace of the country, seeking a spirit which is easier somehow to discover in your land, my country cousin, than in mine. But perhaps I am taking the easy way; perhaps being less than courageous. Perhaps I should look harder here, a greater struggle bringing a greater prize — at any rate, let me hear from you, how the spirit blew through your farmhouse beside the frozen lake on Christmas eve, 1963.

Your city cousin,

Joan

Upon a Midnight Clear

MARGARET LAURENCE

I would bet a brace of baubles plus a partridge in a pear tree that when Charles Dickens wrote *A Christmas Carol* no one wanted to identify with Scrooge, before he became converted to Christmas. How very different now. One is likely at this time of year to run into all kinds of people who view themselves as the Good Guys and who actually try to make you feel guilty if you celebrate Christmas. "It's become totally commercial," they virtuously say. "*We* don't have anything to do with it."

All I can reply, borrowing a word from Scrooge, is *Humbug*. Sure, okay, the stores may less-than-subtly put out their Christmas displays immediately after Halloween; the carols may be used to advertize fur coats or washing machines; the amount of phoniness surrounding Christmas in our culture may be astronomical. But Christmas itself remains untouched by all this crassness. It's still a matter of personal choice, and surely it's what happens in your own home that counts. In our house, Christmas has always been a very important time.

My background and heritage are strongly Christian, although

I reserve the right to interpret things in my own way. In my interpretation, what Christmas celebrates is grace, a gift given from God to man, not because deserved, just because given. The birth of every wanted and loved child in this world is the same, a gift. The birth of *every* child should be this way. We're still frighteningly far from that, but maybe this festival can remind us. Christmas also reaches back to pre-Christian times — an ancient festival celebrating the winter solstice. *The Concise Oxford Dictionary* defines solstice very beautifully — "Either time (summer, winter) at which the sun is farthest from the equator and appears to pause before returning." For countless centuries in the northern lands, this time of year was a festival of faith, the faith that spring would return to the land. It links us with our ancestors a very long way back.

Christmas when I was a child was always a marvelous time. We used to go to the carol service on Christmas eve, and those hymns still remain my favorites. *Hark the Herald Angel Sing, Once in Royal David's City*, and the one I loved best, *It Came Upon a Midnight Clear*. It couldn't have been even near midnight when we walked home after those services, but it always seemed to me that I knew exactly what "midnight clear" meant. I had no sense then that there could be any kind of winter other than ours. It was a prairie town, and by Christmas the snow would always be thick and heavy, yet light and clean as well, something to be battled against and respected when it fell in blinding blizzards, but also something which created an upsurge of the heart at times such as those, walking back home on Christmas eve with the carols still echoing in your head. The evening would be still, almost silent, and the air would be so dry and sharp you could practically touch the coldness. The snow would be dark-shadowed and then suddenly it would look like sprinkled rainbows around the sparse streetlights. Sometimes there were northern lights. My memory, probably faulty, assigns the northern lights to *all* those Christmas eves, but they must have appeared at least on some, a blazing eerie splendor across the sky, swift-moving, gigantic, like a message. It was easy then to believe in the Word made manifest. Not so easy now. And yet I can't forget, ever, that the child, who was myself then, experienced awe and recognized it.

We always had the ceremony of two Christmas trees. One was in the late afternoon of Christmas Day, and was at the home of my grandparents, my mother's people, at the big brick house. There would be a whole congregation of aunts and uncles and cousins there on that day, and we would *have the tree* (that is how we said it) before dinner. One of my aunts was head of the nursing division in Saskatchewan's public health department, and was a distinguished professional woman. I didn't know that about her then. What I knew was that each Christmas she came back home with an astounding assortment of rare and wonderful things from what I felt must be the center of the great wide world, namely Regina. She used to bring us those packages of Swiss cheese, each tiny piece wrapped in silver paper, and decorations for the table (a Santa with reindeer and sleigh, pine-cone men painted iridescent white with red felt caps), and chocolate Santas in red and gold paper, and chocolate coins contained in heavy gold foil so that they looked like my idea of Spanish doubloons and pieces of eight, as in *Treasure Island*.

The dinner was enormous and exciting. We had *olives* to begin with. We rarely had olives at any other time, as they were expensive. My grandfather, of course, carved what was always known as The Bird, making the job into an impressive performance. He was never an eminently lovable man, but even he, with his stern ice-blue eyes, managed some degree of pleasantness at Christmas. The children at dinner were served last, which seems odd today. One of my memories is of myself at about six, sighing mightily as the plates were being passed to the adults and murmuring pathetically, "Couldn't I even have a crust?" My sense of drama was highly developed at a young age.

When the dishes were done — a mammoth task, washing all my grandmother's Limoges — we would make preparations to go home. I always had my own private foray into the kitchen then. I would go to the icebox (yes, icebox, with a block of ice delivered daily) and would tear off hunks of turkey, snatch a dozen or so olives, and wrap it all in wax paper. This was so I could have a small feast during the night, in case of sudden hunger, which invariably and improbably occurred each Christmas night.

The day of Christmas, however, began at home. The one I recall the best was the last Christmas we had with my father, for he died the next year. We were then living in my father's family home, a red-brick oddity with a rose window, a big dining room, a dozen nearly hidden cupboards and hidey-holes, and my father's study with the fireplace, above which hung a sinister bronze scimitar brought from India by an ancestor. I was nine that year, and my brother was two. The traditions in our family were strong. The children rose when they wakened (usually about 6 a.m. or earlier) and had their Christmas stockings. In those days, our stockings contained a Japanese orange at the toe, some red-and-white peppermint canes, a bunch of unshelled peanuts, and one or two small presents — a kaleidoscope or a puzzle consisting of two or three interlocked pieces of metal which you had to try to prise apart, and never could.

As my memory tells it to me, my very young brother and myself had our Christmas stockings in our parents' bedroom, and Christmas had officially begun. We were then sent back to bed until the decent hour of 7:30 or 8:00 a.m., at which time I could get dressed in my sweater and my plaid skirt with the straps over the shoulder, while my mother dressed my brother in his sweater and infant overalls. We then went down for breakfast. In our house, you always had breakfast before you had The Tree. This wasn't such a bad thing. Christmas breakfast was sausage rolls, which we never had for breakfast any other time. These had been made weeks before, and frozen in the unheated summer kitchen. We had frozen food years before it became commercially viable. I guess our only amazement about it when it came on the market was that they could do it in summer as well. After breakfast, we all went into the study, where we had to listen to the Empire Broadcast on the radio, a report from all those pink-colored areas on the world map, culminating in the King's speech. The voices seemed to go on forever. I don't recall how my brother was kept pacified — with candy, probably — but I recall myself fidgeting. This was the ritual — the Empire Broadcast *before* The Tree, a practice which now seems to me to have been slightly bizarre, and yet probably was not so. Our parents wanted to hear it, and in those days it wasn't going to be repeated in capsule form on the late night news. I guess it also taught us that you could wait for what you wanted — but that's a concept about which I've always felt pretty ambiguous.

At last, at last, we could go into The Living Room for The Tree. The Living Room, I should say, was the only formal room in that house. We did not live in it; it was totally misnamed. It was For Best. It was the room in which my mother gave the afternoon teas which were then required of people like the wives of lawyers in towns like ours. The Living Room had a lot of stiff upholstered furniture, always just so. It was, as well, chilly. But it was the place for The Tree, and it seemed somehow the right place, something special.

And there it was, The Tree. *Oh.*

I could see now why we'd been so carefully kept out of the room until this moment. There, beside The Tree, were our presents. For my brother, a rocking horse, two horses cut out of wood and painted white with green flecks, joined by a seat between them. Our dad had made it, for he was a very good amateur carpenter. And for me — wow! A desk. A small desk, found in an attic, as I later learned, and painted by our dad, a bright blue with flower patterns, a desk which opened up and had your own private cubbyholes in it. My own desk. My first. That remains the nicest present that anyone ever gave me, the present from my parents when I was nine.

It was only many years later that I realized that the rocking horse and the desk had been our presents then because no one could afford to buy anything much in that depression and drought year of 1935. And it wasn't until long afterwards, either, that I realized how lucky and relatively unscathed we'd been, and how many people in this country that year must have had virtually no Christmas at all.

One other aspect of my childhood Christmases was Lee Ling. He was the man who ran our town's Chinese restaurant, and he lived without his family for all the time he was there. In those days Chinese wives were scarcely allowed into this country at all. My father did Lee's legal work, and every Christmas Lee gave us a turkey, a large box of chocolates, and a box of lichee nuts. You might possibly say that Lee did it because he hoped to get on the right side of the lawyer. My father wasn't like that, and neither was Lee. The point of this story, however, is that Lee Ling continued at Christmas to give our family a turkey, a box of chocolates, and a box of lichee nuts after my father died, for years, until Lee himself died. To me, that says something valuable about both Lee Ling and my father.

Much later on, when my own children were young and growing up, our Christmases became patterns which reflected my own Christmases many years ago, but with our own additions. We had ten Christmases in our house in England, Elm Cottage, before my children became adults and I moved back home to Canada to stay. Christmas in that house was always something very good and warm, and there were usually a lot of young Canadian visitors there with us at that time.

As in my childhood, the Christmas stockings were opened early in the morning. The difference was, with us, that my kids always made a Christmas stocking for me as well, their own idea. The stockings had candies, including the same kind of chocolate coins, but they also had a variety of joke presents, sometimes kids' books when my kids were no longer children, because we've always liked good children's books and we frequently give them to one another.

Some of the traditions continued. In our house, you always have breakfast before you have The Tree. But in our time, The Tree was in my study, not a "special" place, and we frequently went in wearing housecoats and dressing-gowns and bearing large mugs of coffee. The presents were distributed one at a time so everyone could look at each. We made it last about two hours. I don't think gifts need to be meaningless. I love opening presents from people who care about me, and I love giving presents to people I care about, hoping I've chosen something they will really like, something that fits their own personality, something that will be a symbol of my feeling for them.

Our dinner at Elm Cottage was always fairly hectic. I was in charge of what we called The Bird, as it had been called in my own childhood. I twittered and worried over that turkey, wondering if I had put it in the oven soon enough, or if I was going to overcook it to the point of total disaster. It always turned out fine, an amazing fact when one considers that our stove was so small as to be almost ridiculous and that even cramming a 15-pound turkey into it at all was a major task. The turkey, I modestly admit, was accompanied by some of the best sage-and-onion stuffing in the entire world. Our friend Alice always made her super cranberry sauce, which included walnuts and orange, and was the best I've ever tasted. Our friend Sandy always used to do the plum pudding, which she cleverly heated on a small electric burner set up in the hall, as there wasn't room on the stove. My daughter had been the one to organize the cake, a month before, and everyone had given it a stir for luck. It was a very co-operative meal. Yes, the women did prepare all the food. But the men carved The Bird, served the dinner, and did the dishes. It always seemed to me that our efforts meshed pretty well. Our friend Peter once said that Elm Cottage was a scene of "agreeable anarchy." I think it was, and that phrase certainly describes our Christmas dinners, at which we never had less than a dozen people, and sometimes more.

After dinner, we would move to The Music Room, which was our version of The Living Room, except that we really lived in it. It had a good stereo and a feeling that people could come in and sit around the fireplace and play their guitars and sing their own songs. This used to happen a lot, and always at Christmas. We made new traditions. One of my own favorites was a ritual which said that at some point in the evening our friend Ian would play and sing two songs for me. Corny and out-of-date they may be, but I like them. They were *She Walks These Hills in a Long Black Veil* and *St. James Infirmary Blues*.

Those Christmases at Elm Cottage had a feeling of real community. For me, this is what this festival is all about — the sense of God's grace, and the sense of our own family and extended family, the sense of human community.

Boxing Day

LINDA SVENDSEN

The morning after Christmas, I was in the kitchen picking at cold turkey and reading my new young adult book. It was called *Milestone Summer* and it was all about a teen-age girl named Judy, whose father's death plunges the family into a colorful poverty. She's forced to become a thrifty interior decorator after school and meets Kent, a catch, who's conceited and sails. There were misunderstandings, there were barbecue and pool parties, and I couldn't put it down. It was set in California.

My mother came in scuffing her gift mules. "Is that your brother on the couch?" she asked.

"It's him," I said.

"I didn't hear him come in," she said.

"I did."

"Late?" she asked.

"How late's late?" I said.

"Two."

"Yup."

"Under the influence?" she had to ask. I didn't say anything.

"I guess he was then," she said. She shook her head. "He won't be happy." *He* meant Robert, and my mother had just married him, although they'd been keeping company, laundry and bowling and meals and stuff, since she'd fled my father a few years back. Robert was twelve years her junior. Mom tucked in a towel around the turkey and took it away. "You've polished off all the dark, Adele. You know that, don't you?"

"Sorry," I said. "Like your mules?"

"I'll stretch them," she said. "They're a tad tight. How's the book?"

"Judy had to miss the regatta and Kent stormed off in a huff."

"That's life," Mum said. She wandered out and I heard her in the living room patiently saying, "Raymond. Raymond. Raymond," until she gave up.

I placed the book face down and looked out the window. The yard glared. On the west coast, in Vancouver, we weren't accustomed to snow. Like a long spell of fair weather in summer, it was unusual, worthy of attention and respect, an omen. I watched a tabby cat follow its breath across the white crust. Every few feet, the cat sank, then kept perfectly still and waited for fate. I couldn't tell if it was scared stiff or smart.

Sleep took him away. My brother Ray had a way of sleeping deep that made me jealous. His left eyebrow lifted in a kind of shrug and he smiled, as if privy to an epic starring his truly. I always wanted to see what he saw, do what he did, be where he was. He worked longshoring, was twenty-five to my eleven, and didn't act it. We also had two sisters, Joyce and Irene, who were married and no longer fun; Ray, Joyce, and Irene all shared the same father.

I tickled my brother's nose with a strand of tinsel. He turned to the cushion. "Cut it out," he said. I brushed his cheek. "Cease and desist, Adele, or you will die a slow, painful death." I stopped. He opened his eyes. "Merry X-mas," he said.

"That was yesterday," I said.

"Very funny,"

"I'm not kidding," I said. "I'll tell you what I got, starting with my stocking — "

Ray sat up. "My pants? Where are they?"

"La-Z-Boy," I said.

"Fetch," he said.

I hopped up and brought his trousers over by a belt loop, so I wouldn't empty his pockets. He pulled them up and on. "Mum awake?" he asked. "The *hombre* of the house?"

"Mum's making the bed. Robert's making noise in the shower," I said. "Mum was worried about you. She called the RCMP to see if anybody who looked like you was in an accident."

Ray shook his head. "I'm indestructible," he said. "Where's Dallyce?"

"Texas."

"The girl," he said.

"What girl?"

"I'm losing my marbles," he said. He threw on his sweater, tapped his pocket for nicotine, dug into his jacket, and pulled out car keys on a red rabbit's foot. "Grab your coat," he said. "Let's go quick."

At the drug store Ray bought Mum everything, Evening in Paris, the shebang; Robert, Old Spice deodorant and swizzle sticks, erotic ones, with buttocks and breasts; our sisters and their husbands, Black Magic chocolates, and stole all the ones with nuts when we got back to the Volkswagen. I chose Sea & Ski suntan lotion, which made you look Egyptian any season. It lasted longer than foundation. It didn't wash off. I wanted to fool kids at school and make them think I'd been somewhere. It was the only item Ray had to pay full price.

On the way home from the mall Ray said, "So."

"So?"

"So how's Mum doing? Okay?"

"I don't know," I said. "Ask her."

"You know the dirt. You're the only one home now. She and Robert still fight?"

I nodded.

"About?"

"You yesterday," I said. "How could you forget? You didn't even call."

"Long story." He braked for a yellow and we skidded over the traffic line into the intersection. A truck honked.

"Ice," I said, and he said, "Yeah, ice."

When Ray and I got back, a little whisper I'd never seen before, blonde and maybe thirty, sat at the kitchen table absorbed by Judy's life. Her hands seemed too tiny to hold my book.

"Where's my mother?" Ray asked her.

"Don't know. Nobody was here when I got up," she said. She sounded like she was coming down with something.

"They probably went next door for the open house," I said. "Then tonight we go to Irene's for turkey. It's her turn. We cooked yesterday."

Ray and the lady stared at each other. Then she said, "Lose your manners somewhere?"

Ray planted a kiss in her direction, in air. "Dallyce, this is Adele," he said. "She's the baby of the family. Adele, Dallyce. She's my baby."

"Don't count on it," she said.

"That's the lay of the land, eh?" He opened the fridge door, bent, and disappeared. "Where did you finally crash?"

"Down in the rec room," Dallyce said.

"Comfy?"

"The Ritz it's not."

"Dream of me?" he asked.

"A little hairy," she said, which made him peek at her over the door. I wasn't sure she heard him right.

"Come back down with me and I'll serenade you on the piano. Then you can giftwrap for me."

"Thanks, but no thanks," she said.

Ray cracked ice cubes into a tumbler and poured two fingers of rye. "You both know where I am," he said.

I took off my jacket and hung it over my chair. Dallyce and I looked at each other across the table, and then we heard the opening bars of *Moon River*.

"My song," I said.

"He's not bad," she said.

"Yeah," I said. "You want coffee?"

Dallyce lit up. "Yes, please, thanks."

I filled the kettle and plugged it in. "So have you known my brother very long?"

"Since Christmas." She folded the top of a page in my book and closed it. "You could say I found him in my stocking. Literally."

"Sugar?" I said. "Milk?"

"Both."

We waited for the kettle to sing. "So do you do anything?" I said. "Work, I mean?"

"I teach."

"What?"

"I sub. Substitute. Science, French, P.E., you name it."

"Guidance?"

"Once I taught Guidance," she said.

"Guidance is for the birds," I said.

I poured the hot water and Dallyce came over to doctor the brew. She wore a striped mini-skirt with matching top, something Tarzan's Jane might toss on in the jungle first thing. I looked down. "Hey, you've got the same mules as Mum. My stepfather got her a pair."

"Oh," Dallyce said. "They're hers. I didn't feel like squeezing into my boots." She stirred her coffee. "Ray says your mother's visited the altar a few times, eh?"

"Three."

"Three times."

"She's not exactly an Elizabeth Taylor," I said. "She's had it tough. It didn't work out with Ray's dad, and it didn't with mine."

"How's this one going?"

"Better."

"That's good." Dallyce put the mug down. "I was married once upon a time."

"Oh yeah?"

"Yeah. We got hitched on New Year's Day before the Polar Bear Swim. It was incredibly cold out so we stayed in the car and watched all the crazy gooseflesh make a mad dash for the sea." Dallyce lifted an edge of the towel, tore off some turkey, and ate. She also picked dark. She said, "It's not for everyone. Marriage."

When Mum and Robert trundled laughing up the driveway, Ray and Dallyce were still whispering and wrapping things in the rec room. I was reading, sprawled on the couch, under the tree lights. Robert, the big lug moose, stamped his boots on the front mat, then Mum the moose did. "It's below freezing," Robert said, opening the door. "Colder than a witch's tit."

"Here's my angel," Mum said. "Right under the tree."

"That's no angel," Robert said boisterously. "That's the brat."

"Don't call her that." Mum used her mock hurt voice.

"Why not?" Robert said. "That's what she is — the original brat."

"How was it?" I asked. "The open house?"

Mum slid off her coat and hung it up. "Nice to see the neighbors. I guess."

"Once a year is once too much." Robert lowered himself into the La-Z-Boy. "You wouldn't believe it, Adele. What the Strattons did. Should I tell her what the stupid Strattons did, dear?"

Mum floated back in. "Oh, I don't think she's really interested, hon."

"Sure she is."

"Not really." I pointed to my book. "Judy and Kent are on the brink."

"Hey," Robert stood, crossed to the couch, and crouched by me, his breath in my face. If I struck a match, the air between us would have lit. "And what are Judy and Ken on the brink of? Love? Hate? Wild sex? All three? Will there be a happy ending? Will anybody die? Who did it?"

"Don't torture her, Bob," Mum said.

"Am I torturing you, brat?"

"Yup."

Robert made a sad face, grabbed the last handful of peanuts from the dish on the coffee table, and sat back down.

"Where'd Ray get to?" Mum said. "His car's still — "

"Rec room," I said. "He's got a guest."

"Who?" Robert jumped up again.

"A school teacher."

"A school teacher!" Robert said. "Not a parole officer?"

"A school teacher," I said.

Robert strode into the hall and bellowed. "Raymond, bring your teacher up and introduce her to your parents."

"He's irrepressible," I said.

Mum looked at me from across the room. "It wouldn't hurt for you to take an interest in what he has to say," she said gently. "After all, who's keeping a roof over your head? Who's putting presents under the tree?" And pointedly, "Peanuts in the dish?"

"I was only reading," I said.

"Who provided what you're buried in?" she said. "You

207

know, he would give the shirt off his back for you kids. Does anybody ever think it hurts me to see him ignored?"

I closed my eyes. In the hallway, my brother introduced Dallyce to Robert. "My mother seems to have vanished," Ray said. "She tapped her magic mules together and went away."

"No, here I am," Mum said, and cleared her throat. "I'm right here."

Ray was ages in the upstairs john and Robert was verbal. He was warmed up. "Well, Dallyce. June — Ray's mother — and me — "

"I'm Adele's mother, too," Mum interrupted.

"Yes," Robert said, "June is Ray's and Adele's mother, and since we're being technical, Irene's and Joyce's mother, and what the hell, she's everybody's mother. Happy now?" he said.

"Happy," she said.

"Good. All right. What I was starting to say, Dallyce, was that June and I are what you could call a love match. I've been through a couple of tragic marriages I won't go into tonight. June here has suffered through two. Her first husband busted her heart running off with a Pacific Western airline stewardess, which would be the polite thing to call her. And Adele's Dad . . ." Here Robert glanced at me across the rec room. "Well, how would you tell the story, Adele?"

"I don't know," I said.

He looked at my mother. "How would you describe it, sweeter than honey?"

Mum twisted the glass in her hand. She looked tired. She needed lipstick. "Well, he didn't know how to show affection. You've probably met men like that, Dallyce."

"Sure," Dallyce said softly.

"With him it was always work, work, work," Mum said.

Robert got up to fix himself another drink. He was tall, with a voice big and capable as nature. He lowered it now. "Honey, in fact, wouldn't it be fair to say Adele might not even be here if you hadn't (pardon my being crass, Dallyce), got down to brass tacks? Correct me if I'm wrong."

Dallyce studied me hard as if I was coming and going before her very eyes. My mother nodded and said, "That's true." Then she looked at me and added, "But I would have had you anyway, Adele. Nothing could have stopped me."

"Of course," Dallyce murmured.

Robert went on. "June hoped the baby would save the marriage, you see."

"Right," Dallyce said.

"Now let's drop it," Mum said. "It's Boxing Day."

Ray came back in. "Why's everybody so serious? It's time to —," and he sang, "*jingle bell, jingle bell, jingle bell rock.*"

"Your stepfather —," Dallyce began.

"Bob, please," Robert said. "And let me compliment you on your good taste, Ray." He gave a little nod Dallyce's way.

Dallyce nodded back. "Bob here was explaining how he and your mother got together and that marriage as an institution really works."

"Humbug," Ray said and made me laugh. "Let's party."

"Isn't he something?" Mum said to Dallyce.

I passed around the chips and garlic dip. Dallyce only took a few because she was on the mistletoe diet. Robert said she didn't need to lose. He said if Ray poured mercury into her he could use her to tell the temperature. She said, "Your parents are terrific. They really are the Hosts with the Mostest."

I picked up the phone on the sixth or seventh ring. "What's going on over there?" Irene, my sister, shouted. "My bird's drying out in the oven."

"Ray's here," I said.

"Is he all right? Where'd he blow in from? Mexico?"

"Nowhere," I said. "He's okay."

Irene paused. "Were there words? From you know who?"

"No," I said. "Ray brought a girl."

"Who?"

"A teacher."

"Smart move," Irene said. "Well, round everybody up and get over here. We'll wait for you. Tell Ray to drive carefully, there's a lot of roadblocks, and don't you ride with him. Go with Mum." She paused. "What's that?"

"Everybody's singing carols."

"Who's everybody?"

"Mum, Ray, Robert, and Dallyce."

"Her name's Dallyce?"

"Yup."

"And what are you doing? Nose in a book? Don't say yup."

I hung up and Mum came upstairs and poked her head around the corner. "Who was it?"

"Irene. She's holding the turkey for us."

"We better get going." Mum leaned closer. "Dallyce seems like a nice gal, doesn't she?"

"She's all right," I said.

"You don't like her?"

"I didn't say that," I said. "I said she's all right."

"Her skirt's short, though," Mum said. "Isn't it?" Then she rested her hand against my forehead. "Are you okay, hon?"

"A-1," I said.

She went back down and I went up to the bathroom. I locked the door and took off my blue corduroy jumper and white blouse and slip and underpants and navy blue knee socks. I clipped my bangs back with Mum's bobby pins. I gave the Sea & Ski a good shake, unscrewed the cap, poured lotion into my palm, and applied it thinly and evenly. It was cool. Across my forehead and cheeks, around my nose and lips and eyes, down my neck and shoulders and below, on any bit of me that might ever show. It was like getting into someone else's skin. I waited a few minutes for it to dry.

On the other side of the hill we lived on, there was only a sprinkle of snow. Enough to keep the plastic reindeer, strutting across lawns and roofs, and sleighs, from being ridiculous. It was already pitch dark. Mum wiped the windshield clear with her glove and Ray's vw tail lights blinked at us.

"She looks stupid," Robert said.

"She doesn't look stupid," Mum said. "Why do you keep saying that? She looks like she's just stepped out of a play. She looks made up."

"She looks stupid," Robert said. "Tell me why you did it."

"Don't say again I look stupid," I said.

"Well," he said, "you do."

"Enough," Mum said.

"She does. I'm just curious to know why a half-bright eleven-year-old would do such a stupid thing."

"I did it," I said, "because I wanted to pretend I'd been somewhere else."

"Oh," Robert said. "India?"

I didn't answer.

"Is this meant to criticize me as the breadwinner? Because we can't afford to take holidays like your friends?" Robert asked.

"You're going too far," Mum said.

"Am I?"

"Change the subject, Bob."

Ray made a quick left, Robert followed, then Ray picked up speed.

"That Dallyce seems pretty nice," Mum said. "Down to earth. Maybe she'll be the one."

"A teacher," Robert said. "He probably didn't meet her in the pub."

I piped up, "They met at a mutual friend's."

We drove in silence. Ray made another left, and then we did. The road was dark and bordered by open fields. I remembered my father had taken me to the pony rides there when I was little. I'd sat on the back of Hi Yo Silver, the oldest, most polite pony in captivity, and Dad had led us around, around, and around the winding sawdust path until the pony's bedtime. Now it was a new development.

Robert's signal kept ticking after the turn.

"Ray won't keep a girl like that, honey. A teacher and all. He's got to really shape up. Lay off the booze."

"You think she's better than him?"

He sighed loudly. "Why do you always twist my words, dear?" he asked.

"Am I twisting them, dear?"

"I think so, dear," he said. "What do you say in the back seat?"

"I'm not here," I said. Ray seemed to be going faster and leaving us behind. His tail lights shrank in the distance.

"Sometimes I get the feeling everyone's against me in this family," Robert said. "I really get that feeling." His voice shook.

"Here we go," Mum said. "Deck the halls. Tra la la la la. And do you know the feeling I get, dear?"

"No."

"I get the feeling you could really go for a young girl like that. Wearing bare legs up to there."

Robert glanced over at her. "Take that back," he said.

"Up to heaven," Mum said.

"You'll take that back," he said. Robert laid on the gas and we shot up the road.

Ray slowed, and signalled, and pulled into my sister's driveway. He was unfolding himself from the car, one foot on the ground, as we zipped by Irene's twinkling home. Dallyce must have been waiting for him to jog around and open her door. For a second, I could see what he saw. The Plymouth going dangerously fast; two ghosts in the front seat, my shadow behind.

"Take it back," Robert yelled, and pointed the car at a tall cedar on the side of the road. There was no way we weren't going to hit. We were going to hit. We were going to hit. Off the pavement, on the gravel shoulder, the car sang as Robert edged the wheel and pressed the brakes into a long scream. When the car stopped, our bodies kept traveling forward, then we snapped the few inches back into ourselves.

In the idling car we sat still. No one was hurt. The night was black outside us and the brights lit up the ice. The gauges on the dash glowed blue. He stared straight ahead, breathing rough. In that big cold quiet, she turned to him and kissed him, and kissed again, until she kissed him into kissing, kissing her back, until I couldn't hear the in, out, in again, of our breath.

Notes on Authors

MARGARET ATWOOD is the author of such books of fiction and poetry as *Surfacing*, *Lady Oracle*, *Bodily Harm*, *Interlunar*, and *The Handmaid's Tale*, which has been produced as a feature film. She lives in Toronto with novelist Graeme Gibson.

DON BAILEY lives in Winnipeg with fellow film producer Daile J. Unruh. He is the author of several books of poetry and fiction, including *Sunflowers Never Sleep* and *Homeless Heart*, which won the Canadian Authors' Association Silver Medal in 1989. He has written a biography of his dear friend Margaret Laurence entitled *Memories of Margaret*.

ROY BONISTEEL is the celebrated host of the long running series *Man Alive* on CBC television. He lives in rural eastern Ontario, near Trenton, and writes periodically for the Kingston *Whig-Standard*.

HAYDN BRISLEY is a former police officer who was born in Kent, England and now lives in Anola, Manitoba.

CORALIE BRYANT is an educator who taught for many years in Manitoba and now lives with her son in the Northwest Territories.

DAVID CAVANAGH is a former resident of Eastern Ontario who now lives in Vermont. His work has appeared periodically in the Kingston *Whig-Standard*.

LESLEY CHOYCE was born in Riverside, New Jersey, and now lives in Porters Lake, Nova Scotia. He is the publisher of Pottersfield Press and the author of *The Second Season of Jonas MacPherson* and *An Avalanche of Ocean*, which was nominated for the Stephen Leacock Award for Humor.

MARY ALICE DOWNIE is a renowned children's author and editor who has published such books as *The Wind Has Wings*, *Honor Bound*, *Jenny Greenteeth*, and *How the Devil Got His Cat*. She lives in Kingston, Ontario.

MARIAN ENGEL published ten books of fiction during her lifetime, notably *Lunatic Villas* and *Bear*, which received the Governor General's Award in 1976.

BEATRICE FINES grew up in the Rainy River Valley in Northwestern Ontario and now teaches creative writing in Winnipeg schools and universities. Her stories have apppeared in *Chatelaine*, *The Saturday Evening Post*, *Discovery Magazine*, and *Green's Magazine*.

JOAN FINNIGAN is a celebrated poet, playwright, and oral historian whose work includes *The Watershed Collection*, *The Best Damn Fiddler from Calabogie to Kaladar*, and *Tell Me Another Story*. She lives just north of Kingston, Ontario near Hartington.

DONNA GAMACHE has published stories in *Western People*, *Our Family*, *The Toronto Star*, and *Tales from Canada for Children Everywhere*. She lives and teaches school in MacGregor, Manitoba.

DAVID HELWIG is the author of several acclaimed works of fiction, most recently *Old Wars* and *Of Desire*. He lives in Kingston, Ontario.

MARGARET LAURENCE published many great works of fiction during her lifetime, notably *A Jest of God*, *The Diviners*, and *The Stone Angel*. Her book for children *The Christmas Birthday Story* is a perennial favorite.

JOYCE MITCHELL is a graduate of the creative writing program at Red River Community College. This is her first published story.

BARBARA NOVAK lives in London, Ontario with her husband and two daughters. Her stories for children have appeared in *The Window of Dreams* and *Miss Chatelaine*, while her plays have been performed on stage and on CBC *Morningside*.

JANE RULE lives on Galiano Island in British Columbia. Her book publications include *Lesbian Images, Inland Passage*, and *Memory Board*.

LINDA SVENDSEN teaches creative writing at the University of British Columbia in Vancouver. Her fiction has appeared in *Engaged Elsewhere: Short Stories by Canadians Abroad, Second Impressions*, and *Northwest Review*.

DAVID WATMOUGH was born in London, England and now lives in Vancouver, British Columbia. His book publications include *The Unlikely Pioneer* and *Vibrations in Time*.